EXILE, NATURE, AND TRANSFORMATION IN THE LIFE OF MARY HALLOCK FOOTE

Exile, Nature, and Transformation in the Life of Mary Hallock Foote

MEGAN RILEY MCGILCHRIST

UNIVERSITY OF NEVADA PRESS | *Reno & Las Vegas*

University of Nevada Press | Reno, Nevada 89557 USA
www.unpress.nevada.edu

Cover photographs © iStock/anela (*background, top*); iStock/Ron and Patty Thomas (*background, bottom*).
Cover design by Louise OFarrell

LIBRARY OF CONGRESS CATALOGING-IN-PUBLICATION DATA
Names: McGilchrist, Megan Riley, 1955- author.
Title: Exile, nature, and transformation in the life of Mary Hallock Foote / Megan Riley McGilchrist.
Description: First. | Reno : University of Nevada Press, [2021] | Includes bibliographical references. | Summary: "This book is about exile and transformation. It is primarily about Mary Hallock Foote, nineteenth-century artist and writer, easterner-turned-westerner, but it is a hybrid work—as well as being about Mary, it is about what it has been like for me, a twenty-first-century American expatriate, Californian-turned-Londoner, to find common ground in the life of a nineteenth-century woman." —Provided by publisher
Identifiers: LCCN 2021008854 | ISBN 9781647790189 (paperback) | ISBN 9781647790196 (ebook)
Subjects: LCSH: Foote, Mary Hallock, 1847-1938. | Authors, American—Biography. | Illustrators—United States—Biography. | Women pioneers—West (U.S.)—Biography. | West (U.S.)—In literature.
Classification: LCC PS1688 .M35 2021 | DDC 813/.4 [B]—dc23
LC record available at https://lccn.loc.gov/2021008854

The paper used in this book meets the requirements of American National Standard for Information Sciences—Permanence of Paper for Printed Library Materials, ANSI/NISO Z39.48-1992 (R2002).

FIRST PRINTING

Manufactured in the United States of America

For Kitty, James, and Lucy

Contents

Acknowledgments

DURING THE TIME I SPENT working on this book, I received much institutional and personal support. I am deeply grateful to the Huntington Library, which gave me a fellowship to study the Mary Hallock Foote materials in the James Hague papers during the summer of 2015. The time I spent as a fellow at the Huntington was invaluable for this project. I am also profoundly grateful to the Lilly Library, at Indiana University in Bloomington, which awarded me an Everett Helm Visiting Fellowship, which made it possible for me to spend time examining the Foote and Gilder materials in their collection. I also wish to thank the Lilly for permission to reproduce photographs of Mary Hallock Foote and Agnes Foote. My visits to the Special Collections at Stanford University, though brief, were extremely productive, and I thank staff there for their assistance and for their permission to reproduce photographs from the Foote archives. Finally, I would like to particularly thank Ann Gardiner Brillhart, Mary's descendant, for her generous permission to quote from her great-grandmother's letters and for her enthusiasm for this project.

Copies of Mary Hallock Foote's letters are available in several libraries, among which I have visited the Huntington Library at San Marino, California, Stanford University's Special Collections at the Green Library, and the Lilly Library at Indiana University in Bloomington. (Copies are also available on microfilm at the Bancroft Library at the University of California, Berkeley.) In very many cases, the letters are duplicated in all three places. Therefore, rather than list all three locations, I identify the letters by date and recipient. Where a letter exists—as far as I am aware—at only one location, I have indicated that in the notes.

The artist colonies of PLAYA and Hewnoaks generously gave me uninterrupted time, and peace, to work on my project; the proximity to the natural world in both places was a true gift.

Many individuals have given help and encouragement. I am deeply grateful to all of them. Sands Hall's personal and intellectual generosity and enthusiasm for the project from the very outset has been inspirational. My friendship with Sands is one of the many things for which I have to thank Mary Hallock Foote. Foote scholar and WLA colleague Christine Hill Smith has also been a tireless source of information, good will, and friendship. Ellen Druckenbrod, of the Boise City Library, generously assisted me with research on obscure bits of Foote lore, answered emailed questions cheerfully, and has been an enthusiastic supporter of this project. Along with Ellen, Mary Ann Arnold and Janet Worthington, tireless advocates of the Footes and the force behind the founding of the splendid Foote Park in Boise Canyon, spent a day taking me around Foote sites in and around Boise. Jim and Caryl Tyberg gave me a wonderful place to stay while I was working at the Huntington, and I thank them very much. Chris Duggan gave me invaluable assistance with the illustrations. My friend Steve Coates offered advice and encouragement throughout this project. Two colleagues at the American School in London, Miles Dunmore and Peggy Elhadj, have been unfailingly interested and supportive. I would also like to thank the current and past administration of the American School, which has generously supported my attendance at the Western Literature Association conferences over the years. Invaluable technological assistance was provided by Mariam Matthew, another ASL colleague, and my great-niece Libby Bakke. Their patience with one as technologically illiterate as me has been remarkable. Neil Campbell and Susan Castillo have both kindly written numerous references for fellowships and residencies and have also been good friends. My WLA colleagues, too many to name, have been the source of much support and inspiration, but special mention must go to Melody Graulich, without whose kindness in sharing electronic copies of the Foote letters this project would have been inestimably more difficult and whose scholarly work has been a source of inspiration. David Fenimore has given me much good advice and has become another friend I would never have known had I not met Mary Hallock Foote.

I would also like to thank the University of Nevada Press, and particularly my editor, Margaret Dalrymple, for taking on this project. Margaret's enthusiasm for the book has been great encouragement to me, and her patience in awaiting final drafts kindness itself. And I would be remiss if I did not express my gratitude to copyeditor John Mulvihill, who made this book better.

Researching Mary has taken me on many journeys, during the first of which my daughter Kitty and I spent nearly a week in Nevada City and Grass Valley. On that trip, thanks to the kindness of Sands Hall, I was able to meet Elisabeth Haskell, one of Mary's great-granddaughters. I remember the evening I spent with her and her husband with great pleasure. My first trip to Boise, a marathon car journey with my sister-in-law, Maggie Tracey, was full of serendipity: doors opened as if by magic; the people we met could not have been kinder or more helpful; the project, still in its infancy, took its first few steps.

My large extended family and many friends have been hugely supportive. For fear of leaving someone out, I will not try to name everyone, but first always are my children: Kitty, James, and Lucy. My brother and sister-in-law, Brendan Riley and Maggie Tracey; my son-in-law, Jason Gray; Annie and Rob Caliendo; Clare Statham; and Kate Coyne all deserve thanks. They have picked me up at airports, in the Oregon outback, at train and bus depots and ferry terminals; they have driven with me thousands of miles to see sites, look at archives, visit museums, wander round old mines, and take in the view from the tops of mountains. I hope they all had as good a time as I did! Thank you to all, and thank you Mary for giving us a reason to do it.

EXILE, NATURE, AND TRANSFORMATION IN THE LIFE OF MARY HALLOCK FOOTE

Introduction

In the middle of the journey of our life I found myself
within a dark woods where the straight way was lost.
—DANTE, *Inferno*

The Backstory

I WASN'T SURE WHAT I WAS DOING. I had been researching a slightly obscure Victorian writer and illustrator for several years. I probably knew more about her than most people I actually knew in "real" life. What was I to do with the mass of knowledge I had acquired, and how was I to do justice to a remarkable woman whom I felt deserved more than an academic study?

There was a way of course. The straight way was continuing with perfectly acceptable academic writing that no one much outside of academia would ever read. I have a lot of respect for scholarly endeavor, and have spent a fair amount of my life absorbed in it, but I sensed that my energies might be better used in something that connected to a wider audience than the scholars of western American literature, who, up to that point, had been the tolerant beneficiaries of my somewhat scattershot researches. The dark wood I was in might actually be the path to something vital and important, if I could find my way through it. More personally, I thought that if I found the way I intuitively felt was there, I might get some deeper understanding of my own thinking and of the meaning of my own life and its trajectory.

But there was much more to this than simply a cerebral journey. My life had recently been shaken, very thoroughly and to its foundations; and my sense of a changed world, in which carpe diem was no longer an option but an imperative, was profound. I had been through life-changing events before, but now a near miss with the eternal boatman convinced me that the moment was right to do that which had been asking to be done for some time. The question was, where to begin? I had some bricks and mortar; what kind of building was I going to produce? The rest of my life—my teaching, relationships with my family and friends—would, I hoped, carry on as always. What was going to happen if I wrote this work would happen to me alone, and if I were able to produce something, it would have to stand or fall on its own merits. If I didn't write it (which more and more did not feel like an option), no one would know or mind very much, but I knew that I would feel its absence like something lost.

So, my bricks and mortar.

I had, at a rather late age, earned a PhD and made myself into a bit of a scholar of some aspects of western American literature. This was surprising in that I had been living in England for many years, and up to about the age of forty had not—despite being American—been particularly interested in American literature. I had read the required texts as a student, but my focus had been on Europe. If anything, I had been an aspiring medievalist. I wrote a master's thesis on Middle English poetry and considered going further, only to have my dream deflated by an Oxford don who told me that, of course, one really could not be a medievalist without better Latin than I had. I don't think that particular don meant to drive me from academia, but that was the result, and probably a good thing at the time. I fell into high school teaching when the offer of a job arrived. And so life went along in the way it does, until after a couple of decades and a personal crisis, I rediscovered American literature. That, I guess, was Dark Wood Part I. Doing a PhD and getting back to work led me out of that part of the wood, along with time and the never-to-be-forgotten support of many friends and family members. The way through that dark wood was lighted with love. I was lucky, and I knew it: lucky and blessed.

Dark Wood Part II was perhaps initially less dramatic. After the doctorate, a book, some articles, and enough positive reinforcement to allow me to consider myself a scholar, if a minor one, I began to wonder what the point of continuing with my studies was. I loved doing research and enjoyed writing papers, but I began to question the wider significance of my intellectual life. I would sometimes spend weeks, if not months, researching to produce a paper that might then be heard by thirty people at a conference. It was not that I didn't value the act of writing itself, and the response of those thirty people; it was just that I felt I had more to say and a larger audience to reach. And a topic beckoned.

I had become interested in Mary Hallock Foote, a Victorian writer and illustrator, for a lot of reasons. Mary was born in 1847, in Milton, New York; she died in 1938, in Hingham, Massachusetts. In between those two dates she became one of the most sought-after women illustrators of the nineteenth century, and one of the preeminent artistic interpreters of the American West from the female perspective. She wrote thirteen novels, a memoir, several collections of short stories, many children's stories, and articles for *Scribner's, Century Magazine,* and the *Atlantic.* She also maintained a happy and successful marriage and brought up three children. Mary had married a mining engineer, Arthur Foote, and left New York in 1876 when she was twenty-eight years old. Never intending to, she nonetheless spent most of the next fifty years in the American West.

Mary Hallock Foote had been tangential to my PhD work, and cast a new light on one of the authors about whom I had written. Wallace Stegner had used many of Mary's letters and large excerpts from her (then unpublished) memoirs in his Pulitzer Prize–winning novel *Angle of Repose.*[1] This was disturbing because Stegner didn't identify Mary's letters and other writings as sources, and the reason *Angle of Repose* is a great book is arguably because of the depiction of Mary Hallock Foote, created using her own words and thinly disguised as the character called Susan Burling Ward in the novel. I had written a paper on this topic, ruffled a few feathers, and thought I was finished. Except I wasn't. Writing that paper had led me to some interesting places. But I can see that a bit of background is necessary here.

I first picked up *Angle of Repose* one rainy homesick morning in 1992 in a bookstore in Baltimore. I was living in Baltimore because my husband, a doctor, was working at Johns Hopkins Hospital for six months. I missed London, where we lived, and where I live today. And I missed California, from where I had been gone for nearly a decade—more if I included graduate school and a couple of years in Spain. I had three small children, one in kindergarten, one in second grade, the youngest still in nappies. I was in the thick of it, left to my own devices most of the time. I was at a turning point in my life, though I didn't know it then.

My baby sat in her pushchair as I leafed through a book that had attracted my attention. I liked the cover—a picture of the Sierra foothills in California, which I knew well. I didn't like Baltimore. From the perspectives of London and California, it felt stuffy and small. Used to chatty South Londoners, I found the cliquish parents at the older children's school unfriendly. I missed my London friends, my house, my garden. I felt like a stranger in the country I had always considered my home. Later things would change, somewhat, but just then I felt lost. It was too wet, too hot; our little apartment, which belonged to two young doctors who were staying in our large, comfortable house in London, had cockroaches. Not unusual, we were told. This was small comfort.

So, I was in a state of double exile, among people who ought to have been compatriots but who were more foreign to me than any European ever had been. Neither of my possible personas seemed to work. California, people seemed to despise; London made them nervous. With all these things on my mind that day, I picked up *Angle of Repose*. Opening it, I was suddenly in a well-known world: 1970s Northern California, Grass Valley, the Sierras. And the people: there were lots of Californians I recognized, and a woman protagonist, a long way from home, who wrote a lot of letters. Email was just a rumor in those days, and letter writing was one of my passions. This was my kind of story.

My little daughter was getting restless. I bought the book. And so it began, one exile reading about another.

Mary Hallock Foote, the daughter of New York Quaker farmers, never intended to be a western woman. The Hallocks were broad-minded and educated and believed that women had as much right to education as men. As Mary showed a decided talent for drawing, after she left boarding school the family was persuaded to let her go to New York City, to attend the School of Design for Women at Cooper Union. She lived with her brother and sister-in-law and attended classes while beginning to pursue her career as an illustrator. She was remarkably successful, in time one of the most admired and sought-after women illustrators of her generation. During her years at Cooper, she met many talented and promising young artists and thinkers, but by far the most important friendship she made was with Helena de Kay. Mary and Helena were both dedicated to art, and their friendship was based on mutual interests and admiration, but their backgrounds were very different. Helena came from old New York; she was wealthy, well connected, well traveled, multilingual, and beautiful. There is no doubt that Mary, with her Quaker simplicity and natural diffidence, was more than a little in awe of Helena, regarding her as superior in all ways—although history tells a different story. The two had an intense youthful friendship, which settled into a solid and lifelong bond, carried on for over fifty years through their letters across the continent—sometimes across oceans, as Helena traveled extensively, though strangely never to the West.

After completing her studies at Cooper, Mary's talents began to be recognized, and the commissions came rolling in. It was the age of the illustrated periodical, and Mary was regularly commissioned to draw for *Scribner's,* the predecessor to *Century,* and other notable magazines of the day. She also had commissions for illustrating popular books, including works by Longfellow and Nathaniel Hawthorne, among others. During this heady time, on New Year's Day 1873, she met Arthur Foote, a young mining engineer. Arthur had studied at Yale and was from a background similar to Mary's. He was on his way west to work when the two met. Although they saw each other infrequently during the next several years, they wrote regularly—sadly, few of these letters have survived—and in February 1876 they were married in a Quaker ceremony at Mary's family home. During the same period, Mary's friend Helena had met and married Richard Gilder, who became the pioneering editor of *Century Magazine* and who was to become a critically important influence on Mary's work.

After a few months' delay, Mary went west in the summer of 1876 to join Arthur, who was working at the New Almaden quicksilver mine, near San Jose, California. The couple initially planned to spend two years in the West while Arthur established himself in his field. However, as with so many well-laid plans, things did not work out quite as anticipated. And although Mary did go back to New York fairly frequently in the early years of their marriage, and spent several extended periods at her family's farm when Arthur was working in various inhospitable places, they stayed in the West until 1932.

During their western years, Mary and her family lived in New

Almaden and Santa Cruz; Leadville, Colorado; Boise City and Boise Canyon; and finally Grass Valley, California, to which they moved in 1895 and remained until 1932, when they went to Massachusetts to live with their daughter, Betty. Arthur Foote, though highly competent and even visionary in his field, did not always make the best choices in business terms, and the Foote's financial affairs were often precarious. During these years, particularly when they were living in Idaho, they depended financially more and more on the earnings from Mary's illustrations and writings. She had begun writing sketches of western life during their time at New Almaden and Santa Cruz, and within a very few years became a highly respected novelist and short story writer—in addition to her work as an illustrator, both of her own works and those of other authors.

The Footes had three children, two girls and a boy. Mary was a devoted wife and mother and always considered her children and Arthur her first priorities, but she never believed, as did some of her contemporaries, that marriage and a career as a creative artist could not be happily combined in a woman's life. When the Footes' youngest child, Agnes, died in 1904 at the age of seventeen, of complications following an appendectomy, Mary did not write for over half a decade. When she picked up her pen again, writing became a solace; she wrote five more novels and completed her memoirs.

Mary's dearest friend and lifelong correspondent, Helena Gilder, died in 1916. Soon after Mary's death in 1938, their daughters, Betty Foote Swift and Rosamund Gilder, began planning to edit their mothers' voluminous correspondence with the aim of publishing it. Although they got some way into the project, the work was never completed, and Mary's letters and papers are now mainly at the Huntington Library, Stanford University Special Collections, and the Lilly Library at Indiana University at Bloomington. Helena's letters are primarily at the Lilly.

Most people who know anything about the remarkable life of Mary Hallock Foote know about her—in freely adapted form—from Stegner's novel *Angle of Repose.* The novel begins in the voice of the grandson of the character Susan Burling Ward, a very slightly altered Mary Hallock Foote. The modern sections of the novel are Stegner's, but the retrospective chapters about Susan and her husband, called Oliver Ward, a thinly veiled version of Arthur Foote, follow the exact form of Mary's memoirs, still unpublished when Stegner, then a professor of creative writing at Stanford, wrote his novel. Additionally, there are large sections from Mary's letters in the novel, many verbatim, some very slightly altered. A manuscript copy of Mary's memoirs is housed in Special Collections at Stanford University, as are typescript copies of most of Mary's correspondence. Stegner made no secret of his use of these, but never acknowledged the extent to which he had used sections of both the letters and the memoirs wholesale, possibly thinking that no one would ever look at them again. This was in itself bad enough, since all the sources were used without attribution, but the real-life problem came with the concluding chapters of the novel. Not content with simply "warping"[2] Mary's blameless life of hard work and devotion, Stegner threw in some adultery to spice up the mix, and made Susan—the Mary character—responsible for her daughter Agnes's death through negligence, letting her drown in her father's canal while her mother was dallying with one of his associates. The daughter in the novel was inexplicably given the same name as the real Agnes Foote, who, as I have written, tragically died at seventeen. Ugly, yes. But of course, it was all entirely untrue of the real Mary Hallock Foote.

The problem was compounded by the fact that Mary, Arthur, and their children were so thinly disguised as characters as to be obvious to anyone who had known them, and some characters were not disguised at all, making the novel seem less like fiction and more like a family history. In fact, many people who read the novel with some knowledge of the Foote family assumed that Stegner had unearthed hidden family skeletons. In 1971 there were still plenty of people who had known Mary Hallock Foote, who died in 1938, and the depiction of the character called Susan Burling Ward looked enough like the actual Mary to be taken as such by many people. Enough of the novel *was* verifiably true that this was an easy assumption to make. This effect was enhanced by Stegner's incomprehensible use of Hallock and Foote family names in a work purported to be fiction: Burling was Mary's mother's maiden name; Ward was a Foote family name. Although Mary's children were not still alive when the book was published, her grandchildren were, and the family was not happy with the depiction of their grandmother.

The year following the publication of *Angle of Repose,* the Huntington Library published Mary's memoir, edited by Rodman Paul and titled *A Victorian Gentlewoman in the Far West: The Reminiscences of Mary Hallock Foote.*[3] Anyone could see the similarities, even without reading the letters. Papers were written; voices were raised. But by that time Stegner's novel had won a Pulitzer Prize, largely, it could be argued, on the strength of Mary's own language. And Stegner, considered the "dean of western letters," was relatively untouchable, though his reputation suffered mightily, at least among those who cared about artistic integrity. It is a controversy that has rumbled on for the best part of four decades and shows no signs of going away. Like an underground burn in an abandoned mine, it occasionally bursts into new flame, but by and large smolders away sullenly in the deep shafts of the academic colliery. That's the background to part of Mary's story. However, that is not my topic in this book, though it is a side issue that can't be ignored.

I'd like to go back to that morning in Baltimore when I first picked up *Angle of Repose.* The novel begins in California of the 1970s and is initially spoken in the voice of the Mary character's grandson, a historian, crippled by bone disease, who spends much of the novel railing against modernity. The plot moves fairly rapidly backward from the 1970s to the 1870s and begins to tell the story of Mary Hallock Foote, renamed, as I have said, as Susan Burling Ward.

Angle of Repose immediately appealed to me. I started high school in 1969 and left America for good in 1980. So a book set in the 1970s in California spoke to the need I felt—in 1992—to be connected to my old life. The seventies and California got me reading, but the voice of the character called Susan—a voice that spoke of love, homesickness, exile, and transformation—kept me enthralled. I felt like I was hearing about my own life in someone else's voice. It was Mary's voice, of course, but I didn't know that. Largely on the strength of my admiration for *Angle of Repose,* several years later I decided to write a PhD dissertation, partly on Stegner. So, Mary drew me to the scholarship that became my lifeline in the wake of a private life ever more complicated.

It wasn't until sometime after I had finished my dissertation that I became aware of the controversy surrounding Stegner's use of Mary's letters and memoirs. One summer I spent a few days at Stanford University in the Special Collections reading some of Mary's letters. The next summer I went to Grass Valley, where Mary had spent many years of her life. There I met the writer Sands Hall, who had written a play, *Fair Use,* about the Stegner-Foote controversy.[4] Sands took me and my daughter (the same daughter who had been in the pushchair when it all began!) to see Mary's grave and the house in which she had lived during the later California years. Through Sands's good offices, I was introduced to one of Mary's great-granddaughters, Elizabeth Haskell, who gave me further insight into the roots of the situation. In a fever of indignation, I wrote a paper on Stegner's appropriation of Mary's work and later that year presented it at the Western Literature Association conference in Spearfish, South Dakota.

My paper covered a certain amount of territory that had been traversed by other scholars, but also drew attention to the fact that since Stegner's use of the letters and memoirs, there had been a revival of interest in the life and works of Mary Hallock Foote herself. In reading her letters, I discovered a body of work that went beyond her fiction; there was more to Mary's thought than was revealed in her novels, journalism, or even in her memoirs. Professor Melody Graulich of Utah State University kindly passed on electronic copies of many of Mary's letters, which made my further researches infinitely easier. Two more papers followed in 2013 and 2014, which discussed Mary's relationship to the natural world of the West, as revealed in the letters. Finally, a fellowship at the Huntington Library in San Marino in the summer of 2015 gave me time to immerse myself in Mary's writings, published and unpublished.

It was at about this point that I realized that in some sense I had been leading Mary Hallock Foote's life for over half a decade of my own. I had involved myself so thoroughly in Mary's life and works that I felt I knew her almost as well as I knew anyone. And in some ways her life had become more immediate to me than much of my own. I hadn't, at that point, reread my own letters, yet I had read hundreds of hers—and many of the responses. I had visited places she lived. I had read almost every word she ever published. I had met some of her descendants and many other scholars who had an interest in her life and work. In a very real sense, studying Mary's life had given me a new life; I owe many friends and experiences to my work on Mary. And while she has been considered a minor author, I had seen lines in her writing that shone like those glimmers of bright metal sought by the miners she often wrote of, and these transcendent passages nearly always had to do with her relationship to the natural world around her. I was more and more convinced that there was something very important about Mary Hallock Foote and something that needed to be said. The Stegner debacle seemed to me particularly sad, but only a diversion from the main path. Stegner had made virtually no effort to disguise Mary Hallock Foote in *Angle of Repose*. In fact, the ham-fisted way in which he used the Foote and Hallock family names, as well as using some actual people's names—including those of two of Mary's children—made it seem that he wanted it to be obvious that Susan was Mary.

I was puzzled, but could not help but think that part of the problem lay in the fact that Mary's gentility rankled Stegner. That seemed obvious from the many references to her privilege and the overall tone of the novel. Perhaps that is the reason he did what he did. Or perhaps he was not aware of what he was doing. As a historian, perhaps he felt that unpublished letters and memoirs, even of a well-known author, were fair game. But I am fairly certain that a male author of the nineteenth century would not have received such cavalier treatment. With these things in mind, I decided it was high time that *Angle of Repose* not be the first thing one found when researching Mary Hallock Foote. So, bringing Mary out of *that* dark wood was part of the answer to my own questions.

Correspondences

After I wrote about reading Mary's letters, and not rereading my own, I thought, well, why don't I? So I spent time looking through some of them. I was searching for something in a cupboard where I keep a lot of ancient history when I came across several bundles of letters, which I hadn't looked at since I'd received them. They were not very well ordered, but roughly chronological. I got out the ones my parents had written me while I was in college. Reading them, forty years on, was suddenly like talking to my parents again. How much I hadn't remembered—events, places we went, names of people, many long dead. I've been away from California for longer than I was there. But I never realized, till I reread those letters, that I had forgotten so much. I suppose at some point I didn't *let* myself remember things. I first came to England in 1977, went home in 1978, and then a couple of years later went to

Spain, where I lived for two years. Then I returned to England, and at that point decided to stay. But my homesickness was like a chronic disease, and it was sometimes overwhelming.

Reading Mary's letters had struck a chord. In some of the letters to her friend Helena, her longing for the familiar world she left behind is poignant, a cry from the heart. But she could allow herself such expressions because she initially believed that her husband, Arthur, also wanted to return to the East eventually. In my own old letters to my parents, I can see that I never let myself express my feelings about *my* exile, never let the pain and sense of loss I felt spill out onto the page. I had chosen my life, unknowingly, when I fell in love with an Englishman who had no desire to leave his country. Who was I protecting with those chatty letters, myself or my parents? On reflection, I don't think I could have let myself articulate what I was feeling; it would have demanded too much of me then.

I have not seen many of Mary's early letters to her family, so I can't say whether she let herself express to them the often-complex feelings she had. I suspect not; she too would not have wanted her family, especially her parents, to worry about her. Her letters to her friend Helena, on the other hand, have the quality of a journal; intensely personal and discursive, sometimes they read as though she's talking to herself. Mary relied on Helena to understand her. In looking through the Foote-Gilder archive at the Lilly Library at Indiana University in Bloomington, I came across a revealing letter from Mary's daughter, Betty Foote Swift, to Rosamund Gilder, Helena's daughter, written after Mary's death:

> July 11, 1938
> I must tell you that at the most unhappy time—when she was just herself to know what was happening to her and there seemed to be nothing in life she could bear to think about. I found that any mention of Aunt Helena gave her some relief from despair. I used this fact as one would a strong stimulant, not too often for fear it should lose its strength. It did not, and I think sometimes she used it herself. It got more and more difficult for her to communicate with us. She could still use quantities of words and little phrases and quotations but they were all mixed up and irrelevant and got more so when she tried to fix her mind on what she wanted to say.

> Once when she could not make me understand she said as if to herself: "Helena would have understood." Another time she said: "Helena understood everything."[5]

There is no doubt in my mind that the letters to Helena acted as a kind of "safety valve" for Mary throughout her life.[6] She expressed all her doubts, hopes, and fears to Helena, and then was presumably able to carry on with day-to-day life. But of course there would often be weeks in between Mary's letters and Helena's responses. To say that Helena would have understood belies the fact that it was Mary herself who understood, who made herself understand through the expression she gave her thoughts in her letters. The letters were her inner life: like some artists' practice of "morning pages," the letters kept Mary on an even keel, while keeping her connected to her old life. I think about the importance of writing when I read Mary's letters. And I think too of the fact that the current generations, brought up on email and Facebook, Instagram and Twitter, won't have any such letters to rediscover; their histories are all so visual and immediate. And so much of it will be lost, deleted, left on the old laptop or phone that's been replaced by the newer model. (Or perhaps worse, both good and bad will be kept in "the cloud" for whatever years there are, until the grid finally, inevitably, goes down.) Writing, writing by hand as we all used to do, and then reading those penned writings, either at the time or a hundred and thirty years later, is a very different experience.

I have spent much of my own life writing things down and trying to make sense of them. I have sometimes turned fact into fiction, and sometimes come to believe it. I have written diaries and journals, letters by the ream, stories and poems, articles and essays. My parents were journalists, and writing was the family business; so I wrote and never questioned the process. Writing has been my way into the world.

But Mary was an artist first, a writer later. She had a different project in her writing. Beyond her letters, her writing about the American West was initially to fulfill the expectations of an eastern audience who believed in a geographical wonderland, a land of endless possibility and opportunity, coupled with a sense of eastern cultural superiority. And of course, there *was* a specific type of cultural superiority if one compared the built environment of the East with the unbuilt one of the West and left the environment out of the equation; and Mary was at first entirely in tune with that expectation. We hear that in her early letters. In one written to Helena when she was en route to her new home in California, she says:

> [July 1876]
> I do not care for the towns—they are all alike and *all dreadful*! But the lonely little clusters of settlers' houses with the great monotonous waves of land stretching miles around them make my heart ache for the women who live there. They stand in the house-door as the train whirls past, and I wonder if they feel the hopelessness of their exile. It is somehow the more pitiful because they seem to be in the midst of plenty.[7]

This suggests that while the towns of the West caused her dismay, her sympathy is reserved for the isolated settlers, particularly the women—settlers from whom she no doubt would have kept herself entirely aloof, but for whom she could feel pity. So far, so Frances Trollope-like, and so much to be expected from a sophisticated easterner going west.[8] And even her positive impressions of the western landscape are somewhat predictable, though lovely and evocative, in their descriptive qualities. In the same letter, she continues:

> I cannot tell you how grand it was after sunset last night! Johnny & I were alone on the platform. Johnny fell asleep with his head in my lap, so I had the sunset and the great prarie [*sic*] all to myself—its outline against the sky was absolutely without a single detail to break its magnificent loneliness—a wind blew across it—very strong and yet soft—as if it came over miles & miles of sun warmed fields—The sky was barred with streaks of red that faded and changed at twilight into dark blueish gray phantoms taking the shape of great cannon pointing all one way like a great battery moving into action.[9]

The magnificent loneliness we recognize; and the sky in martial formation is also a familiar trope. And this is how she begins, writing to the East, telling the East what it wants to hear and what it expects. But all that changes later as she begins to live her new life, to understand the natural world of the West and her place in it.

Mary had always had a relationship with the natural world akin to that of the transcendentalists, with whom she had some real-life connections. She was passionate about nature, alive to it in every way. When she moved with her husband from East to West in 1876, it took her some time to fully assimilate to the new world, yet her feelings toward it—though not about the society that went with it—were profound and appreciative. She knew she was in a world that spoke to her in a new language, and she learned that language in her prose and her drawings. As her familiarity with the western landscape developed, so too did her writing about it. Mary's new knowledge is revealed in often luminous prose, which tells of a relationship between a woman and the natural world from a female view that goes beyond the simplicity of gender binaries, and which undercuts the frontier myths and expectations of an eastern reading public.

Mary's language does other things too. It tells the story of the trials of exile and separation: how a cultivated eastern woman dealt with life in what was a raw, relatively untamed West; how she dealt with separation from family and friends; how she managed to create a successful career against all odds in a world where women's careers were not only subject to the whims of men but were also regarded as less important than almost any other aspect of a woman's life. However, her own life and career were blessed by the fact that her husband Arthur was her greatest supporter and advocate.

Transformation

When Mary Hallock Foote, one of the most promising young artists of her generation, left New York at the age of twenty-eight to go west with a young engineer, Arthur Foote, she had known him for four years, but she had spent less than a month with him, if one counted up all the days they had actually been together. But Mary was no flighty young thing; she was a talented, intelligent, business-savvy young Quaker woman who knew exactly what she was doing, and had at least an inkling of what she was giving up. She was already a woman with a sense of vocation and purpose, a large measure of professional success, an abiding passion for nature, huge artistic and literary talent, perseverance of the highest order, loyalty, practicality, and wisdom. She was other things too: a bit of a snob, a bit naïve, a bit intolerant of weakness in others. Some of these things would change during her long western sojourn. Without ever intending to, Mary lived her life in the West, quite a lot of that time longing for the East, but in the end recognizing that she had become part of a new world, and it had become part of her.

Although I consider Stegner's unattributed use of Mary's letters and memoirs indefensible, there *are* some valuable insights in *Angle of Repose*. The first time I read it, I was struck by the transformation of the character Stegner named Susan Burling Ward. Stegner wrote:

> Time hung unchanging, or with no more visible change than a slow reddening of poison oak leaves, an imperceptible darkening of the golden hills. It dripped like a slow percolation through limestone.... [E]very drop...left a little deposit of sensation, experience, feeling. In thirty or forty years the accumulated deposits would turn my cultivated, ladylike, lively, talkative, talented, innocently snobbish grandmother into a Western woman in spite of herself.[10]

When I read those words, which so beautifully articulate Susan/Mary's transformation, I sensed their truth but I felt something else. I was struck by the parallels with my own life: my life, but with the values reversed. I left California in my twenties and ended up in England, in a world that represented all those things that Stegner's character Susan—and the real Mary Hallock Foote—would miss when she went west: sophistication, erudition, worldliness. Those were things I thought I wanted at the time. But in the end, I missed my Californian world—which I realized was not so unsophisticated after all, and which had some things that were irreplaceable, among which was a sublime natural world that, for me, has never been equaled. And of course, what one also misses about the place one is from is simply that: it is where one is from; the place from which one's being, at least in its original form, emanates. Home is a complex concept. In fact, one spends a lot of time trying to evade or erase it. One tries to become something else and sometimes succeeds. I believe what Mary wanted was to become the accomplished artist she became, but equally, she wanted a happy and loving family life. She was ambitious as a young woman, and her home in Milton, New York, where she returned after her Cooper Union years, did not particularly conflict with the person she saw herself becoming. On the other hand, going west with her young husband did. And yet it was in the West that she had her greatest artistic success and her literary career: something she had never dreamed of. In that decision to go west, with all its ramifications, we see what Stegner refers to as her becoming "a Western woman in spite of herself." But of course, she became something else unexpected; she became one of the foremost chroniclers of the American West from a female perspective, both in artistic and literary terms. She told the story few others had: the woman's West. She hadn't expected that when she stepped out her door and began the long journey to self-actualization. Mary's lodestar was Arthur, and the West was where Arthur Foote made his life. So Mary went west, carrying, in addition to her luggage, the printer's blocks for *The Scarlet Letter,* which she had been commissioned to illustrate.

When I made the decision to leave my homeland, for some of the same reasons as Mary, I missed a lot of things. But I didn't have the experience Mary had; I was younger, and no one had asked me to illustrate *The Scarlet Letter*! So, burdened with no printer's blocks or professional acumen, just a humble master's degree in English and a few years' teaching experience, I also set about the task of reinvention in the cause of love. But I particularly missed the nature with which I'd grown up. Of course, there's nature in England, really wonderful places, but it's not quite the same. One can't help being imprinted with what one has known as a child. I positively ached for California live oaks and sun-browned hills, the Sierras, and my much-loved Pacific. I longed for a kind of freedom that at that time, during the early 1980s, seemed to exist in the West because it *was* young and new—or at least newer than a lot of places. But in fact, a lot of that freedom, I now know, was simply youth. Youth gives one such a lot of illusions, but they are durable and hard to escape. But that idea of the *slow percolation* of change that Stegner refers to in his description of the character based on Mary—that happens everywhere, not just in the hot dry hills of Northern California where Mary eventually ended up. That percolation that Stegner described, the way life changes one, resonated for me when I read it, like the English church bells I had grown used to hearing, "change-ringing."

I have now lived in England, a cool, damp, moderate sort of place, for the best part of four decades, and I think the Californian I had been was changed into someone perhaps a bit less lively, a bit more thoughtful than I'd been, a bit more cultivated, and yes, I am ashamed to say, at times a bit snobbish. Like Mary who had wanted to retain her eastern persona but became western, in spite of myself—my Californian self—I became English.

That's not to say either of us went entirely out of character. Mary did not become Calamity Jane, or anything near. She retained her well brought up manners and behavior. Perhaps she lost a bit of the snobbishness she had acquired in her New York City days. But had it been snobbishness when she referred to her friends as the brightest and best?[11] Wasn't that just the arrogance of youth? And in any case, wasn't it partly true? She knew most of the young artists and literati from her time at Cooper Union and through her society friends, the Gilders. Her friend Helena de Kay had married Richard Gilder, soon to be editor of the influential *Century Magazine,* two years before Mary married Arthur Foote. Mary herself soon was numbered among that same group of artists she had admired: her illustrations appeared regularly in *Scribner's* and other notable publications, and her skills were sought after by contemporary authors. (And within a very few years, her writings too would appear next to those of such luminaries as Edmund Gosse, Frances Hodgson Burnett, Mark Twain, Emma Lazarus, and Brett Harte.) But Mary's decision to go west was not reckless; she knew what she wanted. As well as being a hugely talented artist, she was in love, and she wanted to be married; she wanted a family. It is evident from Mary and Arthur's correspondence, and her comments to Helena about her marriage, that she and Arthur loved each other deeply.[12]

Mary was a thoughtful, talented, serious artist, a writer-in-waiting, with an abundance of discernment that would grow into wisdom. She was also a devoted wife and mother. These things need not contradict one another, given the right woman and the right man. And with the support of Arthur, she continued to become one of the nineteenth century's most sought-after illustrators of western America. She had the kind of life women fight for now and dream of having: artistic fulfillment within a loving supportive family. But she had it at a cost, and that cost was what she sometimes called "exile."

What else did Mary become, despite her desire to remain at a distance from western life? What did the West make her? That's part of what I wanted to find out when I began studying her. And I guess a great deal of my quest was personal. I often wondered what my life would have been had I not left California when I did. What I have written about Mary is partly true for me. The parallels struck me at the time: the friends and family left behind; the death of parents, six thousand miles away; only arriving home in time for funerals. Mary even missed the funerals. Flying across oceans today is simpler than cross-country travel was then.

And reading about Mary's life made me realize that I hadn't gone entirely out of character either. England, no one will deny, is a more reserved sort of place than California. And so am I. I like the fact that no one mechanically tells me to have a nice day when I leave a shop in London. If they say it, they probably mean it. I like the dearth of personal questions from absolute strangers. There's a lot I like here. My point is this: although at some level I have regretted living in England, at another, it suits me. But I've made it suit me too, because here is where I am. I suppose what I'm trying to say is that wherever you end up, if it's not where you are from, you are changed in some very deep way by the experience. Mary was. I was. You, Reader, may have been.

One of Mary's novels in which she depicts how a person is changed by a place is *Edith Bonham,* a sort of wish fulfillment written after the death of her dear friend Helena Gilder. In the novel, Ann (the Mary character) dies, and Edith (the Helena character) comes west to raise Ann's child. Edith is changed by the choices she's made, but she's changed principally by the place, and she's changed by choosing to become an exile from the world she knew. Through the character of Edith, Mary is telling her own story. In this novel, we get perhaps the truest sound of Mary's voice. At one point in the story, Edith is in quarantine with Ann's daughter, who has scarlet fever. It was an experience Mary went through with her own children, and the experience depicted might be Mary's own:

> Those six weeks on the mesa were the most searching experience of my life, and their consequences spread over many years that followed. As the mesa lay out there under the bare sky, so was I exposed and sorted and winnowed and beat upon in the glare of a mortal mistake crueler than many a crime. And as the shadow of the mesa at sunrise and at moonrise extended far across the valley, so over the subsequent levels of my life the shadow of that

> six weeks extended. . . . The main thing about it to me then, was its isolation and elevation, in a stripped, stern way, above the whole plain of my former existence.[13]

I don't suggest Mary had made a mortal mistake she was expiating during her years in the West, but the sense of the landscape that "exposed . . . sorted . . . winnowed . . . and beat" the character Edith is close to some descriptions of religious experience, and this is the kind of experience Mary had, and felt, during her western years. The conclusion of Edith's thoughts in this novel are so haunting, they are like a prayer:

> Lightnings and thunder come with the storm, and words are torn from us in the tempest-times of our lives, and dead words we wish had died unborn choke the old paths of memory and mark with waste the track of the storm that is past. But when the clear, dark nights of stars return,—our stars that we see from that "top of the world," as we call the mesa,—or the white nights that steep the earth in moonlight; when the long days of summer's fruition are back with us again and the shortening days bring back the ancient sadness of the harvest-burdened year, we do not complain of these seasons of blessedness that they are not prolific of sound. And so my story, that began late as a love story, must end as the happy love stories do end—in silence: as life shall end for us all at last.[14]

This quiet resolve is something that came, as it does to all of us, through long years of living. I am struck, as I am always struck when I chance upon these diamonds in Mary's prose, with the connection between her deepest feelings and her life in nature. She cannot express those feelings outside of nature: they belong to the world in which she has chosen to live.

This is where I want to say that in her response to the natural world Mary was transformed by the West. Mary was always alive to nature. But in the West that sensitivity was heightened. She was in nature so much of the time, and in a natural world that in its intensity and sometime strangeness eclipsed the world she had known growing up, the much-loved, much-lived-in Hudson River Valley. She had come to a land that spoke a language she did not yet know, a landscape she had to learn to read; but learn she did, and in that learning she understood the wisdom of a place that had been speechless in her world. She understood it, and she shared it: in her drawings, her journalism, her fiction, and her letters. But Mary's connection with nature was always at the center of her being.

Consider this early letter to her friend Helena, written when she was still unmarried and living with her family on the farm in Milton:

> October 12, 1873
> I wrote to Charley [de Kay] a long account of Big Pond the place where we camped one night in Sept. with Charley Farnham. A blissful time we had—almost too nice to describe! There was a waterfall that would have thrilled you through & through with delight. Nobody seems to know anything about it. Charley Farnham took us there by indistinct trail through the woods. We heard it calling to us—blowing its trumpet from the steep—suddenly the trees stopped on the brink of a wild stream, where we scrambled down a bank and crossed over great white boulders trimmed with soft black moss like velvet. The water was clear as crystal and had lovely yellow brown lights in it. There was such a roar & rush & whirl of water that we couldn't hear each others [*sic*] voices except as we spoke face to face. Like the stream we seemed irresistably [*sic*] borne along in a gay excitement to the brink—There we stopped in wonder & gazed at each other in a "wild surmise." Why had we never seen this before—What a pity we could not stay longer—that it was so far from home! There is no use describing a waterfall. I lay flat on the edge of the rock and looked down and under the fall where the water had hollowed out a dark cave behind the white vail [*sic*] of spray. Bessie told me afterwards that she called to me to come away—but I didn't hear for the roar. There was no danger—Arthur Foote held on to my feet (not a joke) and it was the most fascinating thing to watch the water's descent from the shining edge—lit up with sunset into the shadowy ravine.[15]

While this is much like many other descriptions of attractive outdoor scenes, Mary has an eye and gives it drama, with Charley leading them through the woods; and romance, with "Arthur Foote"—clearly a newcomer on the scene—holding her feet while she dangles, physically, and, oh so metaphorically, over the precipice of her future. Nature here is benign and beautiful; a little bit dangerous but not truly threatening; not like the world she will come to know.

During the process of writing this book, I received a fellowship to PLAYA, a creative residency program in eastern Oregon, not far from where Mary lived in Idaho. This was my journal entry for March 31, 2017:

> I stopped writing, or rewriting, I should say, two weeks ago. Two weeks ago, I was in London, sitting at my desk, surrounded by my life in books, my life in culture and history, family and friends. My life.
>
> Now I'm sitting in a wooden cabin looking out at a lake that speaks to me of eternity: 250 miles from where Mary spent the most trying time of her life, the Boise River Canyon. My view is beyond sublime, and not everyone's idea of beautiful. Bare stripped land and sky; leafless trees in vivid light. This vista turns me back to my own thoughts. I think I am in the most pure place I've ever been. Like Mary was in the Canyon in Idaho, or on the Mesa: the drama of land and sky, on which we struggle to impose meaning. I've been gone from home two weeks today. And look where I am! Out here. Out here on the Playa. In the Oregon Outback, miles from anywhere. The silence! The birds! The peace—only occasionally broken by a car or truck on the two-lane highway. The first day was a state of continual epiphany. Now it's slightly different.
>
> Is this how Mary felt, there in the Canyon in Idaho, 250 miles east of here? She was never quite alone—there was always Arthur, the children, the help, the engineers. I wonder if she felt more solitude when she was in her busy Quaker village back in New York? Or in the silent meetinghouse? But even with all that, there's something about this quiet world that must have made humanity disappear. One is nothing, in all this space. One is a dot under the sky; one is a grain of sand next to this timeless lake that seems like an ocean. Timeless. I never understood what that meant till now. This place I'm in: time means nothing here. It doesn't matter. Not at all. I spent an hour watching the sky go from dark to light this morning. One might have visions in a place like this. See God. But I have the feeling one doesn't see God as one might expect. I feel

> like maybe this IS God. This stillness. This quiet. This peace. The long even lake in front of me, the dark low mountains, punctuated by a distant, dormant volcano. Dormant, not dead. I won't want to talk about this place. What can I say? A long shallow lake. Lots of birds, dry grasses. Unremarkable mountains. Sky. Long white clouds. Yellow trees, just waiting for spring. Some slightly more dramatic mountains off to the right. Primeval. Distance. Space. Quiet. The beating heart of the world. But beating quietly. I don't want to die, not at all, but if I did, now, I feel like it wouldn't matter.

I realized when I wrote that, more than I ever had before, that this is what being in the remote places of the natural world can give one—this heightened awareness of things. If it did that to me in a month, think of Mary, out in unmodified nature for most of her adult life!

What's been interesting for me during this process is the fact that in studying Mary, reading her books, reading her letters, looking at her pictures, visiting the places she lived, thinking about the conflicts in her life, I've understood things about my own life. I'm not Mary, though I have persevered in a place to which I'm not native. I think the thing that change and exile and longing can do, when they don't crush you, is to reveal the inner self, what remains when other things are lost. I think that happened to Mary. I hope it happened to me. Perhaps I see parallels where they are not. But there is something in these words that Stegner gives Susan/Mary in *Angle of Repose* that resonates for me:

> Don't you know how we lose the sense of our own individuality when there is nothing to reflect it back upon us? These people here have so little conception of our world that sometimes I feel myself as if I must have dreamed it.[16]

Of course, they are Mary's own words; Stegner has merely appropriated them. What Mary actually wrote in a letter from New Almaden was this:

> October 21, 1876
> You cannot imagine what an intensity is added to all my pleasures of that kind by the setting of this unique loneliness. It is quite different from any loneliness I have ever experienced or imagined.

> I do not feel it when we sit together in the evenings by fire or candle-light, but all the long hours while Arthur is away, I know that I am lost—don't you know how we lose the sense of our own individuality when there is nothing to reflect it back upon us. These people here have so little conception of our world that sometimes I feel myself as if I must have dreamed its existence, then again, for days it seems as if this place and life were a dream, that my being here is one of those incongruous situations which we can accept only in dreams.[17]

The complexity of Mary's understanding far outstrips Stegner's simplistic binary: Stegner's Susan feels her past to be a dream, the present the only reality; what Mary says is that as the past seems like a dream, *so too* does the present, and the acceptance of the present is posited on the fact that its reality is questionable. This gives a depth to Mary's thinking that Susan's lacks. More profound too is Mary's sense that she is lost in her present, that it is a wholly *other* medium of being, not simply an alternative life but a completely new existence that somehow contravenes, without cancelling, the past, the previous reality. This is a profound difference; it's a more dynamic concept than simply overwriting the past with a new story.

It is this sort of dynamism that Stegner misses when he makes Mary into the somewhat pathetic figure of Susan Ward in *Angle of Repose*. And yet it is the kind of story one might write for oneself in weak moments, thinking of one's own exile, or perceived exile. It is the kind of story I wrote on the walls of that library one carries around in one's head, when I felt that choices I made were not entirely my own. Living in a new place, one has the sense that one may, indeed must, reinvent oneself since the old self is out of reach, like a figure waving from a distant shore as the ship pulls away from the land, smaller, smaller, and finally gone.

I sometimes think about my own behavior when I first came to live in England, aged twenty-one, having read everything about everywhere and been nowhere at all. However, it's a different story, for different reasons. I remember being embarrassed by my American-ness, my western-ness, my lack of experience, my lack of cynicism. More than forty years on, I look back on the child I was. The child was as old as she had ever been, and I have to respect her efforts. However, my problem was that I was in love with culture. And I thought knowing the right things to say meant that a person understood things. How wrong I was. That was a dark wood too.

I knew that in her life Mary knew a lot about dark woods, and I hoped that writing about Mary's life might guide me out of my own. So, I decided that in addition to writing about her books and letters, which had been my original plan, I would write about how learning about Mary Hallock Foote had affected me. And then I truly began to see my way.

CHAPTER ONE

In Exile

IN ONE OF HER EARLY NOVELS, Mary wrote:

> When an eastern woman goes West, she parts at one wrench with family, clan, traditions, clique, cult, and all that has hitherto enabled her to merge her outlines—the support, the explanation, the excuse, should she need one, for her personality.[1]

"Explanation" and "excuse" are interesting terms to choose, as though one's personality was something for which one had to make amends, or at least explain. In this, Mary was ahead of her time, acknowledging that the rough edges of one's personality may have quite a lot to do with the contrasts between where one was from and where one found oneself.

When she plunged into her western adventure with Arthur Foote, despite her concerns about the lack of culture in the West, it was clear that Mary knew her own mind and was full of hope. But it was a huge wrench to leave her home. Besides having to contend with the contrast between nineteenth-century California and artistic and literary New York, there was also the loss of the familiar life of the family and farm in Milton. But she was in love, and as anyone knows who has made a change for that reason, the warm haze hides many things that will appear later on. This kind of struggle is fairly common in our age of displaced people, though many transplantation choices are made for less happy reasons than Mary's. We live in a world in which people reinvent themselves in new places all the time. Yet this reinvention often requires the suspension of disbelief. If one knew what would be endured and required, would anyone willingly go through displacement? Many people have no choice in these matters. But to talk about Mary, and myself, I will limit my thoughts to those who chose, willingly, to make a change. In this sense, Mary has become more current than she might have imagined, with her depictions of the feminine interpretation of the West, and her stories of women struggling to find ways to integrate into new landscapes, if not new societies. For Mary's characters, like Mary herself, were often keen to retain their difference from the social world around them.

It was in the natural world that Mary's literary creations most often found themselves comforted, understood, loved. But it is in the natural world as well that many of her characters meet their ends. Mary thus reveals a constant ambiguity inherent in western life, critiquing the mythology of the romantic West, which offered so much but required sacrifice and suffering, and sometimes life itself. Mary's literary world was a dangerous place, as Mary's own western world sometimes was too.

There are further cultural and historical parallels, and one can often see the correspondences between some of Mary's women, both drawn and written, and classical heroines, who so often found freedom in transformation into some aspect of nature. It is a dubious kind of freedom to be changed into a spring, like the classical figure Arethusa, or a tree, like Daphne, but it represents liberation from male domination. With some of Mary's female protagonists, we see a choice made in which nature represents a kind of freedom, even if that freedom is death. We see this particularly in the stories set in pioneer Idaho, in which women often face a choice between moral ruin and an inexorable natural world.[2]

In *The Land Before Her,* Annette Kolodny writes of pioneer "fantasies" of the West, suggesting that men and women wanted different things and imagined different things in the West.[3] This was not often depicted before Mary's illustrations of western themes, including illustrations of her own writings beginning with "A California Mining Camp," which appeared in *Scribner's* in February 1878. It opens with a description of the author picking "a cluster of white-petaled flowers that seem the very expression of the freshness and briefness of the morning." This is immediately contrasted with the fact that "in some shadowy 'labor' a thousand feet below, a gang of Mexicans finishing their night-shift may be passing the 'barrilito' from one grimy mouth to another."[4] The point of view is focused on the kind of minute detail one may characterize as feminine in its emphasis and classical in its overtones, as Mary must have been aware.

In this vision of the miners' underground life in contrast to that of the woman among the flowers above them, the reader hears an echo of the story of Persephone, daughter of the goddess Demeter, who was carried down to the Underworld by Hades—thus transforming the landscape of the New Almaden mining camp into a mythic meadow in ancient Greece. (The remote beauty that New Almaden even now retains—thankfully saved from development by its designation as a California state park—makes the comparison a fitting one.)

These echoes of antiquity are typically nineteenth century. If one looks at the tables of contents of issues of *Century* or *Scribner's* from the time, there are often pieces on classical themes. Glancing through *Century* for 1881 and 1882, one finds titles such as "The Hellenic Age of Sculpture"; "The So-Called Venus of Melos"; "Costumes in the Greek Play at Harvard"; and "Oriental and Early Greek Sculpture." The educated nineteenth-century American woman and man would have had the ancient world in front of their eyes a good deal of the time. It is no wonder then that Mary should use the world of the ancient Greeks as a touchstone in her own descriptions of her new world. However, I believe that there is another reason why the ancients appealed so much to her. The bedrock of Greek thought is Homeric poetry. I think Mary's sense of herself as a wanderer in new worlds would have resonated with the story of Odysseus. In *The Victorians and Ancient Greece,* Richard Jenkyns writes, "The Victorian fancy was recurrently haunted by the ancient world."[5] Mary Hallock Foote was very much of her time, and the West, even while she saw it with new eyes, would have brought to mind those visions of the ancient world that her age used as a template for both strangeness and grandeur.

As Kolodny suggests, Mary and Arthur Foote might have wanted different things, but each wanted what the other did as well. This is what initially seems so promising about Mary's western adventure: she went—rather protected, certainly—with a man who allowed her to see the West as few women had seen it. She was not a slave to domestic labor, as so many were, and therefore she was able to see the West with a female view that seems very modern. Arthur's decency meant that Mary could experience the West as a thinker and an artist. He was always convinced of her worth, and even superiority to himself; he had no presumption that his wife should be his servant. Mary did not need to protest about her rights; she had them without question, and in a relationship where her husband felt no ambivalence about his wife's success. (This may explain why in later life she did not entirely understand other women's need for freedom. In fact, she opposed women's suffrage, for fear it would damage the integrity of the family and make women into wage slaves.) So, initially, Mary's western exile was relatively benign. Yet, it was still exile. Edward Said, himself an immigrant, has written:

> Exile is strangely compelling to think about but terrible to experience. It is the unhealable rift forced between a human being and a native place, between the self and its true home: its essential sadness can never be surmounted. And while it is true that literature and history contain heroic, romantic, glorious, even triumphant episodes in an exile's life, these are no more than efforts meant to overcome the crippling sorrow of estrangement. The achievements of exile are permanently undermined by the loss of something left behind forever.[6]

Said goes on to discuss how, in contemporary thinking, *exile* has achieved a kind of noir glamour. He asks, "If true exile is a condition of terminal loss, why has it been transformed so easily into a potent, even enriching, motif of modern culture?"[7] He continues:

> We have become accustomed to thinking of the modern period itself as spiritually orphaned and alienated, the age of anxiety and estrangement. Nietzsche taught us to feel uncomfortable with tradition, and Freud to regard domestic intimacy as the polite face painted on patricidal and incestuous rage.[8]

This suggests that exile is not always a bad thing, in that it might remove one from potential threats to the self. For example, to cite another western woman writer, some of Willa Cather's exiles *from* the West remove themselves from situations of emotional and intellectual suffocation, such as in the story "Paul's Case," in which the eponymous protagonist goes toward the estrangement of the city despite foreknowledge of his consequent death. But in the time Mary was writing, most American "exiles," particularly women, would have been very specific about their loss, leaving the known world of the eastern states for the unknown West. However, Said refines the notion of exile: "The difference between earlier exiles and those of our own time is, it bears stressing, scale: our age . . . is indeed the age of the refugee, the displaced person, mass immigration."[9]

Similar tenets applied to westward migration in America. Although Mary belonged intellectually to the world that might have found the romantic side of exile appealing, certainly there were those among her eastern associates who believed that for all its romance, and John Muir's rhapsodic essays in *Scribner's,* the West was still beyond the pale, and that she had thrown her lot in with those who, a century later, Cormac McCarthy described as "itinerant degenerates bleeding westward like some heliotropic plague."[10] And although Mary was what Wallace Stegner considered a privileged immigrant, he makes it clear in *Angle of Repose* that she was an immigrant nonetheless. But as Said notes, it is a question of scale. Well-off professionals like the Footes were going to have a different western experience than the masses of westering pioneers equipped with only high hopes and a Winchester rifle, traveling westward in a covered wagon on a wing and a prayer.

Immigration has become a wholly different concept in our time, one with political overtones and agendas, heartbreaking in its human cost. Exile also has a different significance, but the two terms overlap. While westward migration was considered an adventure by some, for many it was not dissimilar to the experiences of hapless immigrants today, as is clear in many accounts of early pioneers.

Mary regarded her husband's professional colleagues as the elite of the western immigrants, yet as an exile from her eastern world of culture and family, she defined much of her being by what she was *not.* There is no doubt she found many of her fellow immigrants, even those of a similar status, socially unacceptable. For example, she did not associate with the wives of the other mining officials in New Almaden. They must have thought her a terrible snob, but she felt that they were from another world, distant from her own. This was not snobbery based on money and associations, but rather a kind of intellectual separateness. As she noted in her reminiscences, she kept herself apart from her neighbors just as her Quaker forebears in New York had.[11] She must have suffered from loneliness, unwilling to mix with others not out of pride but rather out of a true reluctance to be with those with whom she felt there was no common ground. Perhaps partly as a result of this aversion, she spent many hours writing letters to those she had left behind in the East. Yet despite it all, there were compensations in her life, principally nature and Arthur's happiness, which was a source of deep satisfaction to her. She describes this in a letter to Helena:

> October 21, 1876
> Arthur says he can never get used to—"coming home to you." He sits sometimes, in the evenings, looking at me and at the little room, warm and bright in the firelight, and says—"Do I really belong here, with you?"
>
> You know he thinks nothing of himself—or rather he thinks himself a part of the rougher side of creation—a man meant for hard work and the society of other men; and of course he exaggerates what he considers my refinement, by constantly contrasting me with his daily surroundings—I am glad of every pretty and graceful thing we have around us, for his sake—for he *needs* to be refreshed, after coming out of the depths of that grim old mine. His delight in our little dinners lunches and breakfasts—(simple enough, but nicely served, thanks to Lizzie, and to all the good friends who gave us our pretty silver) was quite pathetic at first—he said his meals used to be a "series of skirmishes with 'Mother Fall's' Chinamen."[12]

And a few months later, she writes: "Arthur is always comparing with fresh wonder (and, I fancy a kind of tender pride & thankfulness) his present life with the old time."[13]

There is more in a similar vein. My point is simply that Mary initially dealt with her exile, most of the time, with gratitude for the joy she felt in her marriage and the pleasure she took in the new natural world in which she immersed herself, not complaining about what was missing. Nonetheless, the distance from her familiar world was a constant countermelody to the new music of her life.

Early on in her western sojourn, Mary wrote to Helena:

> September 3, 1876
> I follow Arthur wherever I can—to his office in the morning—and on survey days I go with the party—Arthur, Hastings, Henwood, "Ephraiham"—and the two timber-men, to the Randol Shaft-house, and watch them down into the mine. It gives me a strange feeling to see them go down into that underworld. The men's heads

> show above the top of the "Skip"—the bell strikes, the engineer moves a lever the great wheels slowly swing round and the heads disappear down the black hole—I can see a hand waved and the glimmer of a candle for a little way—the spark grows fainter and a warm, damp wind blows up the shaft. Stranger [her dog] and I go down the trail together and there is a long day all alone. Lizzie is here and she is a good creature but she is not company. I draw in the dining-room and when I am tired of sitting, walk up and down the piazza—one side looks out on the road and the hillside—this I do not care so much for unless I am watching for Arthur to come home, but I love to turn the corner and find myself face to face with the mountains and the valley—
>
> A damp, soft wind always meets one here—It is a peculiar wind—a drying wind, blowing over miles of sun-baked land—and yet cool. I hear it round the house while I sit at work—flapping the shades—stirring the live oak boughs that rest against one side of the house.[14]

As Arthur enters the Stygian realms of the mine, Mary is left above, a kind of willing Persephone, her only real companions the mountains, the valley, and the wind. I wonder how Lizzie would have felt if she'd heard herself described as "not company." She herself was an eastern woman who, with her baby, had come west with Mary to work for the Footes. But Mary was educated far beyond Lizzie, or anyone she was likely to meet in the West, except some few of her husband's eastern engineer colleagues. Times were different, and while this sort of distinction between women of a similar age, from the same part of the world, and both a long way from home may seem strange now, it was part of the social order Mary had known in the East. Mary was unlike most people she encountered in both education and worldview. She wrote people off, deciding quickly who was, and was not, worth knowing. Who knows what she missed with her wholesale disregard of what she saw as spurious western gentility? Strangely, it was women who drew her greatest opprobrium. I wonder why? Did she judge all others by the same standards she judged herself? I suppose foreignness in the other gender is simply taken for granted, but when one is deeply connected with one's own gender, alienation from it is much more painful. I think Mary must have led a lonely life much of the time because she could not lower her standards to connect with those from whom she felt alien. But her separateness came from deep in her nature. As she wrote to Helena in the same letter, "people wear upon me more than I can tell you."

I believe Mary's separateness had less to do with social status than with education and cultivation and, principally, temperament. She and her family had always felt different, even from their Quaker neighbors. This was true with individuals, but initially this sense of distance extended to the landscape as well. She gives voice to this in her character Edith Bonham, in the eponymous novel, who when she first comes to the West states, "I began to feel such a castaway, so foreign to my kind about me, that merely to hear the sound of my own voice again I asked a question."[15] In this excerpt, Edith is traveling westward by train; the landscapes oppress and confuse her. Mary may have felt the same way, although she would grow to love her western landscapes and often spoke of how she knew she would miss them one day. But in the novel, Edith really is an exile, much more so than Mary ever was. Virtually orphaned, she arrives in Idaho to find that the friend whom she has come to see has died. When she sits, stunned, on the edge of the platform, her feet in the soil, she refers to Idaho as "my home." The terrible irony of this new home soil being the same soil in which her friend has been buried does not escape the reader. Nor, one assumes, does it escape the character, whose misgivings about coming to the far West are now fulfilled.

This scene asks the reader to explore how one acquires familiarity. We all know the feeling: arriving at the holiday house rented sight unseen, the first day one feels bereft. It's all been a terrible mistake. We are lost. It is hopeless. Everything is ruined. We wish we had never come. We will pack and go home—in the morning. But in the morning the sun is shining. We get used to the leaky faucet and lumpy beds, and by the end of the week the house is an old friend. We like the view. We will miss the walk from the house to the village shop. Letting go is suddenly hard. We realize, as we close the car door, that we have a new friend in this old house—perhaps not a friend we want to spend our holidays with every year, but the place has become something known. And just as her character Edith acquires familiarity with a new state, Mary Hallock Foote did so with a whole region; a landscape became familiar to her in a way that made life livable—not just livable but full of all life. In many ways, this happened because Mary was alive to the landscape, allowing herself to be won over by it: she who had been brought up in the Hudson River School of representation became the outstanding illustrator of western scenes, seeing them with the eyes of the female realistic painter.

In one of her early short stories, she described a protagonist who, like Mary Hallock Foote herself, was an eastern woman gone west:

> She was gazing down into the valley, as one looks at a landscape who has not yet mastered all its changes of expression. Its details were blurred in the hot, dusty glare; the mountains opposite had faded to a flat outline against the indomitable sky.[16]

This is Frances Newell in Mary's story "In Exile," but it could be Mary herself. That she felt herself to be "in exile" is unquestionable. What is significant is how she dealt with the exile's role. That telling phrase "mastered all its changes of expression" tells one that Mary would, in fact, master the changes of the landscape, would come to know them in such a way that the landscape would become her consolation for the people she had left behind. Mary dealt with her exile not quite by becoming a western woman, but rather by knowing the western landscape: becoming aware of that which was beyond difference—the deep, sometimes inexpressible reality of a new world.

Although there was often a romantic plot in her stories and novels, the longer Mary remained in the West, the more realistic her writing became; this realism came from her own experience. Neither her fiction nor her illustrations of western scenes validated the despoiling of the landscape, or adhered to the grand frontier themes so beloved by both a naïve reading public and the mass of male writers and artists who employed western themes. Rather, she observed the many vexed and difficult choices westerners had to make. Of course, articulating this awareness may have augmented Mary's sense of exile, constantly bringing it to the forefront of her thinking. And the fact that her husband, Arthur, was a mining engineer, and so responsible for much environmental depredation, must have affected her.[17] While she later wrote to Helena about her homesickness, I doubt very much that she complained about it to Arthur, supportive spouse that she was. Her letters to Helena allowed her to maintain her equilibrium in situations often less than ideal.

When Mary began writing novels and western sketches, encouraged by the enthusiasm of both Helena and her husband, Richard Gilder, she offered a new vision of the West to an eastern readership more accustomed to viewing the West through the tired tropes and sentimental settings of the dime novels. This vision grew throughout her career, as Mary herself became reconciled to her own state of exile and grew to love the natural world of the West. Another passage from *Edith Bonham* is typical of the quality and tone of her later descriptions:

> I was extraordinarily happy that night—so happy I couldn't stay in bed. When the moon had crossed the zenith to the side towards the valley and her light came in through the high west windows and struck upon the wall above Phoebe's bed, I took a blanket and stole out of the door onto the back veranda. . . .
>
> Out at the far end towards the north one saw dim hills where the canal-line cut its way through, making a white gash. Eastward the plain that joins the mesa went back in desert land or ploughed land returned to desert; at night the mountain-line withdrew, the whole earth disappeared as it were and the sky was paramount. Stars, millions of stars, and the great soaring path of the Milky Way amazingly white and sown with sparks of light defying the moon. The wind blew soft and steady. . . . The five dead poplars, which must have been quite trees when they were planted, whisked about in the night-gale like witches' brooms. It wasn't beauty—it was a lofty loneliness that resembles the sea, far inland as we were. I began to feel how people who have lived in such places can never go back to the old values of life in villages and towns; they must forever be the "gypsy-souls," homeless in the paths of men.[18]

This excerpt reveals the depth of Mary's understanding of the scene's spiritual and emotional resonance as well as her own place in between worlds, like that of so many of her female protagonists. This understanding of the landscape and natural world is seen throughout her writings, from her earliest missives home from the West to her final memoirs, written in old age.

However, as the author and playwright Sands Hall has noted, there was clearly a significant tension in Mary's western existence, despite the opportunities it offered. This is perhaps the heart of the matter: Mary missed the East, but there was much about the West she loved. And in certain ways, even her "exile" must have appealed to her need for solitude. (Of course, one is never alone in a house full of children, as Mary was for much of her western life.) Hall describes Mary's life as

> camping trips, sunset gallops, excursions into wild geological territory—while Helena was having tea with Mrs. Roosevelt and dinner with Henry James, Mary took enormous pleasure in the options the West and life with Arthur, offered. In an 1884 letter to Helena, she writes of hurtling down the Boise river at night: "The worst that could have happened was the boat might have struck a rock going with the force of that tremendous current and gone to pieces and we would have been obliged to walk home ten miles in wet clothes." Mary knew such opportunities would be impossible in the staid East that nevertheless she longed for so deeply. This friction between what the West gave her and her anguish at "losing" her East, forms a line of tension throughout most of her writing. The Gilders, looming in the background, represented all she'd left behind; they caused almost compulsive comparisons, especially during the Footes' harrowing decade in Idaho. Even as she was becoming known as a pre-eminent western writer, in the juxtaposition of East versus West, West came up lacking.[19]

But though the West may have been lacking in certain ways, Mary knew its value and its power, despite the conflicting claims of her life and her desire to stay emotionally connected to the eastern world she had left. Living in the West was a kind of exile, but an exile she had chosen and one that offered much, particularly to a lover of the natural world, as Mary so eminently was.

Seeing Landscape—A Personal View

Looking at a landscape one has not yet "mastered" is in many ways a liberating experience, for in the lack of mastery lies the possibility of new understanding. I thought about this a lot when I spent a month at the Huntington Library in San Marino in 2015. I was there through the generosity of the library, which gave me a fellowship to continue my researches on Mary. There I was looking at a landscape that was in some ways utterly familiar to me: the arid vegetation of Southern California. It has been many years since I lived in California, and when I did live there, it was not in the south but the more temperate northern region where I was born. Yet I know the weedless, dry soils, the succulents and cacti, the thorn trees and stunted evergreens. Where I live now, I spend whole days fighting the encroachment of every sort of vegetable life. If I don't watch out, tendrils of ivy will grow up the side of my house, digging their roots into the rain-softened mortar between the bricks, loosening slates, crumbling wooden window frames. My garden becomes hopelessly overgrown within weeks of any relaxation of vigilance. There, in Southern California, where I was thinking about these things, relaxing vigilance just means everything dies—desertification is just a few days of drought away.

When I was researching at the Huntington Library, my life was out of time entirely. I spent my days with the nineteenth-century letters of a long-dead author; I walked in gardens where palm trees and ancient statuary stood next to each other. When I left the library and went home, I swam in the dark in the swimming pool outside the door of the house where I stayed; I woke in the early mornings and swam again as the light made its way through the California live oaks. The cicadas played an accompaniment to my typing. Where am I? I asked myself. How does this all exist? I wondered. I was in Arcadia. With reference books. Double Arcadia. I got used to being peaceful, something else I owe to Mary.

Southern California is a different world from the north. The cars are fast, but slowness somehow pervades the atmosphere. I would sometimes find myself driving at a crawl along wide, palm-fringed streets where every house is different but all are the same. It's all so much itself and so much not the north, not the East, not the West, not the rest of the world. LA noir. Yes, I can see where that came from. I can see how all the blue and white and green and yellow equals black: so beautiful, and still it doesn't seem real at all if you come from somewhere else. I felt strange being there; belonging, but somehow alien, something Mary felt so many times in her life.

At several points in her life, Mary found herself in landscapes not terribly dissimilar to the one I saw from my chair by the window at the

Huntington. But she came from a place not unlike where I live now, green and fertile, wet and cold at the right times of the year: hot when it should be hot. When she saw those parts of her new western world, she must have thought how strange the world looks when we see it through eyes not accustomed from an early age to its differences. What was that experience like? I wondered. And how did her experience in the West mediate her vision? From early in her western sojourn, her letters give some indication of the process she was going through. This 1876 letter describes her first impressions on her trip west:

> July 18, 1876
> The scenery on the journey became too grand in the last few days for postal card descriptions...the awful solitude of the Alkali desert—its primeval desolation—one cannot imagine it ever to have been any different.... It was just after sunset when we passed the Great Salt Lake—the mountains were darkly outlined against a vivid sky—the great expanse of water without motion is very impressive—It was a still evening and there was scarcely a ripple over all the lake. The Echo & Weber Canons are beyond words—but you can imagine how fine in color great masses of rock of a deep, sulphurous reddish yellow—more red than yellow towering against an intensely blue, sleepy afternoon sky—with white fleecy clouds. The sun illumined their strange crests but down below the color in shadow was wonderful.... After that came the winding descent into the Sacramento valley—then the San Joaquin plain—all one color, with far off glimpses of water and whirling clouds of dust.[20]

In this letter, Mary initially resorts to rather predictable superlatives—"too grand," "awful solitude," "beyond words"—to describe these inspiring vistas, using literary forms that suit the Hudson River School of nature study. Later in the letter, however, we hear her own artist's voice:

> [We] had tea on the piazza facing the most wonderful sunset—the clouds of dust rolling up from the valley below were transformed by the light into level bars of colors like a horizontal rainbow sweeping across the entire valley—above it the grand mountains rose—a wonderful variety of constantly changing color made them look like something unreal—and as if that were not enough there came

> a sudden darkening of the lower part of the mountain so that the sun lit peaks seemed to float in the air above the level bars of the sun-colored dust, with a strip of cool shadow between.[21]

I like the very specific imagery of "level bars." It takes very little time for Mary to begin to know and personalize the western landscape. This is one of the letters that became "A California Mining Camp," which appeared in *Scribner's* in February 1878. The following passage from the article is probably a combination of Mary's original prose and Richard Gilder's edits:

> Early morning in New Almaden is worth getting up betimes to see. Sometimes the valley is like a great lake filled with billows of fog,—pearly white billows, tumbling and surging with noiseless motion. It is more as if the clouds had all fallen out of the sky, leaving its blue intensity unbroken, and heaping the valley with fleecy whiteness. On windy mornings, the fog rolls grandly out to sea along the defiles of the triple chain of hills; when there is no wind, it rises and drifts in masses over the mountains, making the clear sunlight hazy for a moment before dissolving into it. After the rains, when the morning air has a frosty crispness, the mountains are outlined in sharp, dark blue against a sky of reddish-gold; even the tops of the distant red-woods may be traced, 'bristling strange, in fiery light,' along the horizon. As the sun lifts its head, the dark blue hills flush purple, long shadows stream across the valley, the windows and spires of San José sparkle into sight, and the bay reveals itself, a streak of silver in the far distance. There is no chorus of birds to break the stillness.[22]

Although Mary did sometimes tend toward the purple in her prose, this bears a certain editorial stamp. Mary's letters generally tend to be more personal:

> September 24, 1876
> These mountains are beginning to have a strange, human expression as I watch them day after day—I do not love them as I used to love our little Hudson River hills. They are stern brooding giants—they make a great barrier along the horizon like the tents or

> fortifications of an immense Army, and seem to hold us prisoners—Last night they were wonderful, in the pink sunset light but they always seem to give me the same feeling, whether dark with cloud shadows or gorgeous in sunlight, as of a silent, irresistible Fate—waiting there, patient, unpitying, eternal.[23]

The pathetic fallacy here is appealing. Mary has truly given herself to nature like a nineteenth-century Artemis. It's this giving human emotions to nature, and making it human, that is so appealing in Mary's writing. She has become the place she has moved to; she's internalized it in such a way that she can almost speak *for* it. Even by this early stage in her long sojourn, Mary's perceptions have begun to mitigate her sense of exile and to offer an alternative way of seeing.

Reflection

I was at PLAYA in eastern Oregon, looking at some mountains across a great expanse of lake and thinking about Mary's letter. That sense "of a silent, irresistible Fate—waiting there, patient, unpitying, eternal" of which she writes to Helena is exactly right—although my mountains seemed to me less "unpitying" and more *indifferent* to humanity. "We remain," they seemed to say, "while you pass away like dust in the wind."

Nature sobers one and frees one of any thought that anything we do matters in the long run, unless perhaps we manage to do something really good, or absolutely monstrous. Even then, the effects last only a generation or two before vanishing. Yet the mountains will continue their endless watch, the seas will roll, the sun will rise and set, while we spin endlessly round it, among stars as indifferent to us as we are to a grain of sand among all the grains of sand on the beach.

And perhaps equally sobering is transplantation. To leave our native place requires all our perceptions to become new: requires us to become new. When I was at the Huntington, as I looked out the window at the Southern Californian landscape, I thought of how much I had changed living away from the country of my birth. When I went to England, I was used to brown California hills in the autumn, the drama of the Sierra Nevada, Yosemite, the Pacific coast: a young world that seemed to be still forming. The earth shakes in California. You never feel very secure, but you don't worry about it too much.

When I left California I went to a world in which everything seemed old. Almost everything *was* old, though old did not necessarily mean beautiful. I was homesick. I longed for California live oaks and hawks soaring overhead. I never saw the shed skin of a rattlesnake on any of my damp country walks. I missed heat and dust and California poppies as much as Mary missed ice-skating and dogwood and maples and mourning doves. I didn't know how to read the physical landscape—or the cultural and architectural landscape either. Although I hadn't lived my life totally in nature, in California one is surrounded by it. Nowhere is so urban that you don't feel nature's hand some of the time. In England, it was different. Unless you live in the actual countryside, spaces can feel very occupied. At least the places I lived in did. When I first arrived in England, I lived in Oxford, a city of ancient buildings, water meadows, little rivers, and endless ghosts. Then I lived in a country village—country walks through centuries-old churchyards, romantic little rivers you couldn't swim in, thatched pubs with dark rooms and dark beer. Now I have lived in London for more than three decades. There is a lot of green here, but one is nearly always aware of the weight of centuries of human life. You never step on a piece of ground that hasn't been stepped on ten thousand times before. You walk through ghosts every minute of every day. Every day in the city I walk past places where some of the most significant events of history happened. I'm so used to it as to never be surprised anymore. (My English self gets more of a shock when she's driving the LA freeways, or walking in Yosemite. But like Mary, I'm bicultural now.)

In California, one felt like life was new—I felt that in 1976. How must it have seemed to Mary in 1876?—like the first day of creation, and she the new Eve. It was only "polite" western society, such as it was, that drew her disapproval. People were the problem, not the land. But beautiful landscapes were not enough, and missing her old world and old friends, while glorying in the new, created a Gordian knot that she never satisfactorily undid.

But Mary knew that a new world required a new way of looking at things. She says this very clearly in an undated letter to Helena, sent sometime in the spring of 1878 from Santa Cruz:

> [Spring] 1878
> I wish I could do justice to all we see here. It saddens me that so much must be trusted to memory. I have made one sketch of the

> Santa Cruz beach—only one as yet because of numberless reasons—the chief of which seems to be that one must get acquainted with a place in the spirit of it—before approaching it. All I see here is so strange to me that I cannot attack it at once.[24]

This sense of the integrity of the landscape, that the landscape has a spirit that must be known, draws Mary close to transcendental thought. In her respect for that which she does not yet "read," we hear the Emersonian maxim that not only words but things are emblematic, and "every natural fact is a symbol of some spiritual fact."[25] I am reminded too of a Quaker dictum that Mary would have known: "Spiritual learning continues throughout life, and often in unexpected ways. There is inspiration to be found all around us, in the natural world, in the sciences and arts, in our work and friendships, in our sorrows as well as our joys."[26] Although there was no Quaker meeting where she was, when she went west, Mary's formation was profoundly molded by the Society of Friends. It is from this spiritual connection Mary makes to the landscape that some of her most profound thinking, and writing, comes.

In a letter to Helena dated only Saturday, April 1882, we see further complexity in Mary's developing understanding of the western landscape, which is far from her Hudson River School antecedents. She sees a land in which the mystery of its very being demands simple recognition and acceptance rather than active connection: the antithesis of the frontier spirit in which the frail men entering "these solitudes" with their "flimsy accompaniments" reveal how little humanity actually matters in the face of the natural world:

> April 1882
> The snow peaks, with the shadow of the opposite range climbing their sides at sunset, leaving their gleaming sierras in sharp light against the sky. The lonely trail winding wearily—lost, reappearing—disappearing at last—Enfolding in the long spurs of the range descending into the valley—vanishing at the entrance to the pass. There is an awful temerity in the advance of a handful of men with their flimsy accompaniments into these solitudes—"The desolate land and lone." It has no human history. There is something appalling to me in the blank silence of those immeasurable unrecorded ages that lie there exposed—No *not* unrecorded, but *I* cannot read

> their dumb tablets of rock—I only feel the sphinx-like calm which seems to ask how you expect to live there—If you cannot answer the problem, retreat or death are the alternatives and it makes no difference to anything earthly there *which* you choose.[27]

In this letter Mary's intuitive understanding of the world achieves an acceptance of a landscape that must have initially appeared as foreign as Mars, and which indeed is not livable in this instance. But what strikes me about this passage is not valorization of the landscape, but simply understanding and acceptance of a place "with no human history." Mary's understanding of the West at this point in her long western sojourn accepts that there are other histories than human history. The thoughts in this letter also anticipate a respect for the landscape that was certainly not common during Mary's lifetime, when the natural world of the West was still seen as an inexhaustible resource, open to all takers.

Nature in Exile

In the West, Mary chose nature over society. Nature *became* society; nature became the repository of some of her deepest feelings. It spoke with a voice she could hear and became the company she missed. It became what her friends, family, and culture had been: a source of inspiration and solace. Consider the following letters to Helena from early on in Mary's Idaho years, before hard times hit (when her husband's irrigation scheme fell apart owing to the loss of financial backing), in which she describes the land she lives in.

> March 8, 1885
> The Mesa runs out like a peninsula, long and rather narrow, the valley being the ocean—on the north are the foot-hills running along down in lessening lines to where a far off white peak . . . shows like a great ice-berg looming up—On the south are the Owyhee peaks covered with snow, forming a continuous but more broken range than the foothills. The west is so far-off where the line of the foothills becomes one with the plain that it has much the effect of an ocean view, especially with the far off white peak like a dream of a ship under full sail. I am quite inchoherent [*sic*], for it is fresh in my mind, and brings back so many other places where we have

> been happy that it gives me a strange pang of remembered joy as well as of anticipation.... I know it would rest you, soul and body, to breath[e] that pure strong virgin air—and look over those miles and miles of land that has never been sown in sorrow and reaped in disappointment.[28]

The imagery of the ship under sail is especially evocative: Mary was a traveler in spirit as much as body. She saw things as they essentially were, not as they appeared to be. And there is a way in which that far-off peak *is* a ship under sail. There is a way in which all our perceptions are but images of the spiritual nature of things. The Greeks saw spirits in trees; Mary sees ships in distant mountains. Metaphors speak to us so profoundly because we sense their intrinsic truth. Mary's conviction that "it would rest you in soul and body" reiterates the sense she has of a personal relationship with a sentient nature. The following letter expresses something similar.

> May 28, 1885
> This is a place of strange and wondrous refreshment to me in the outdoor life. Whatever is going on—a moonlight night, a sunset, a great wind, or a day of brilliant sun, you are always *in it*—You see it and feel it and breath[e] it and nothing interferes. Betty was a long time in my arms going to sleep last night and I was tired and heated through and through and depressed. I went down on the beach in the moonlight for an hour, as far from the door as the road at the foot of our yard, at home, and was instantly wrapped round with coolness and softest light and obscurity and a sound of water breaking on the "ripple" and sweeping inshore in long surges—It is so resting.[29]

Mary shifts from the baby in her arms to herself being in the embrace of nature. She is wrapped round with "coolness and the softest light," as nature does for her what she does for her child: consoles, comforts, protects, cherishes.

But nature is not always so benign, of course, and Mary was aware of that. In her 1901 novel *The Desert and the Sown,* Mary gives this speech to the tragic and lonely Packer John, a man whose only mate has been the wilderness:

> "I never *see* nature till I came out here. I'd seen pretty woods and views, that a young lady could take down with her paints; but how are you going to paint that?"—he waved his tallow-stick towards the night outside. "Ears can't reach the bottom of that stillness. That's creation before God ever thought of man. Long as I've been in the woods, I never get over the feeling that there's *something behind me*. If you go towards the trees, they come to meet you; if you go backwards, they go back; but you can't sit down and sit still without they'll come a-creeping up and creeping up, and crowding in."[30]

In this passage, the wilderness is not so much malign as it is *other*—strange and unknowable, truly "creation before God ever thought of man." Similarly, in the short story "Maverick," the hapless Rose, whose bleak life has been equated with the Arco Desert where the story is set,[31] chooses to escape her own hopeless situation by embracing annihilation in nature, wandering into a trackless waste of lava beds.[32]

Nature is clearly two sided in Mary's understanding, but she gives nature agency even in its savagery. Consider this passage from her 1892 irrigation novel, *The Chosen Valley:*

> The face of the plain was featureless and wan. There is but one color to this desert landscape—sage green, slightly greener in the spring, and grayer in summer, with a sifting of chrome dust. In winter it is most impressive under a light fall of snow, not heavy enough to hide the slight but significant configuration of the ground, yet white enough to throw into relief the strange markings of black lava, where it crops out, or lies scattered, or confronts the traveler in those low, flat headed buttes, so human, so savage, in their lone outlines, keeping watch upon the encroachments of travel.[33]

This much is clear: the colorless plain has a face, has a will, and a desire for stasis. Its monochrome being makes demands on the traveler, telling those who journey through its territory that its will takes precedence, once again emphasizing the provisional nature of humanity's tenure in the natural world.

In the following passage from her historical novel *A Picked Company* (1912), one sees Mary's frequent fatalism about nature and its collusion with what she regards as ancient "savages."

> As he stepped forth, facing the burst of distance seen from the divide, he took a fresh breath of amaze. For uncounted centuries all this astonishing beauty had been waiting here for the first white man to behold. Savages had known it and hunted each other off that prehistoric stage. All these covert paths of loveliness had been paths of death taken by predatory feet—"the wolf that follows, the fawn that flies." This stillness was an ambush, and he, crunching through the pure frost, spoiling shapes of wonder at every step, was walking in these invisible footprints, bound upon the ancient trade.[34]

Like the ancients, Mary saw sentience in nature where others of her time saw mere matter. Believing in a creative spirit, she believed in the integrity of all creation, and yet she was aware of the ambivalent *otherness* of nature, its inexplicable, profound reality, beyond good, beyond evil, but true to itself. In this passage, the ambivalence is clear: "paths of loveliness" are "paths of death"; peaceful "stillness" is "ambush"; the walker is "spoiling shapes of wonder" by simply being in this natural place. This is not as simple as romanticism. Mary has a profound understanding of the fact that nature has a being and presence of its own, invisible to those who will not see but utterly real to those whose eyes are open.

The Nostalgia of the Exile—A Personal View

I'd like to briefly leave the open places of nature and get back to the dark wood. My own dark wood had a couple of sources, as I have said. The first was wondering what my academic work amounted to. The other was wondering if my own life as an exile should change at the particular crossroads I'd reached. I'd been an expatriate for most of my adult life. Everything I'd done in terms of marriage, children, and career had been done in England. Like Mary, I often felt nostalgic and longed for the other place—but at that stage, it was mainly the landscape I missed. Of course, I missed friends and family, but unlike Mary, I got to see them regularly. She would leave knowing she wouldn't see people for years, if ever again. And so she wrote to them, and for them, to keep them close. Letters were her salvation; through them she kept herself connected to her old life.

In her wonderful book *A Field Guide to Getting Lost,* Rebecca Solnit talks about losing the person one used to be and becoming someone else;

how the old life is like clothes that don't fit anymore.[35] I like this image, and it reminds me of how Mary, who loved clothes, wrote about turning frocks during the lean years, and darning elbows, making clothes over. This seems like an appropriate metaphor for Mary's life in the West: making the old clothes fit the new person.

I remember a stage of my life when I might be walking down a street or sitting in a classroom, and I'd run through a sartorial litany in my head, thinking something like, "I bought my shoes in Florence. My coat is from San Francisco. I got this sweater in Oxford fifteen years ago. My jeans are from when I lived in Spain." It connected me back to those places, knowing I was wearing bits of them.

I think, too, of how I have returned, more or less every summer for the past thirty-plus years, to my childhood home across the Atlantic. As much as I like going there and being in California, it feels strange to be back in a place that is so full of memories of the first years of my life. Being in such a deeply lived-in place takes me emotionally back to the age I was when I lived there. I am never so aware of myself as a child as when visiting my childhood home. But I remember my teenage years and early adulthood too. It's not quite nostalgia. I don't want to be ten again, or even twenty. Maybe thirty, but by thirty I was six thousand miles away, in another life.

Nostalgia, it's a strange condition. *Nostos:* returning home from a long journey. Returning home is what Odysseus longed for; it's what Mary longed for; and I did too. But home changes. And there's the other half of the word: *algia:* pain or illness. So the sight of the blue Californian skies, the live oaks, the arid landscapes, and plants that like the aridity, or at least put up with it, is that which is longed for but causes pain at the same time. It's not home anymore. Home is wet and rainy, and a tall brick house on a London street. But this other, old world *feels* like home: home if I'd lived some other life. And so one goes round and round, wondering what might have been, or perhaps what *is* in some different realm of being.

I, too, became an exile. Exile. Émigré. Refugee. Expatriate. Those are Edward Said's terms. One becomes all these things when one leaves home, but new things too: citizen, denizen, dweller, never quite native but naturalized. Becoming natural: being part of nature: being part of the new nature of a new place. Is that what happens?

And now I've become naturalized in the life of someone else—Mary's life has been part of mine for the past ten years or so. More. I find myself considering things the way she might have done. I find myself wondering how she might have regarded my life, so privileged in culture, yet as a city dweller so poor in nature.

Mary was an exile, separated from a close-knit family and life, but that family had been in exile too, separated from their Quaker kin by choice and circumstance. They were mild Quakers with backbones of iron that were not as unforgiving as they were definite in their choices. An anti-slavery uncle offended the congregation; so the congregation lost the uncle and family. Mary came from a determined lot and was used to choices of conscience. It was a good thing she had the principles she did, considering the situations Arthur Foote found himself in and in which he demonstrated a similar moral compass.

As part of this study, I spent some Sundays sitting with the Quakers. Mary brought me to that too—what a lot I have to thank her for! The thing I felt most in the meetings—the sitting in "expectant silence"—is that after a while the inner eye opens. Maybe it doesn't see a lot, but it begins to. And I think it was this openness that Mary brought to the West—to her perception of nature in the West.

In the Huntington Library, I read Mary's memoirs as she had typed them—her own mistakes (few) and her granddaughter's notes. I felt like I was with her as she went to New York—only seventeen—on such an adventure. And I followed her travels, back and forth across the continent, in a time when travel was not easy and farewells often meant forever—leaving one world and arriving in another wholly new. They can be the making of people, these departures and arrivals, but the marring, too, when they happen too often, go on too long, lead back to nothing but further absences and questionable goals.

I remember being twenty-one, arriving in England on the first flight longer than an hour I'd ever been on, coming for a year to a place I'd never been. But then, I'd never been anywhere but up and down the West Coast of the United States. I remember the strangeness, yet weird familiarity. Everyone spoke English, and I was well read for a twenty-one-year-old, so I recognized things that had lived only in my mind before then. When the bus from the airport—no Underground connections into London in 1977—pulled into Reading train station, I wondered where Reading Gaol was, where Oscar Wilde had written his ballad.

Later that day I found myself in Oxford. Found is the right word to use, for I really felt like I had been delivered on a magic carpet into some fairyland, all golden stone buildings, everything I saw as old as anything I had ever imagined. The first few weeks in Oxford are something I don't think about too often: the beginning of the huge change in my life that would take me away from California and make me into someone new. It gives me a slightly panicked feeling to think about the decisions I was going to make after that particular magic carpet ride, and what life might have become if I hadn't arrived, if I hadn't stayed. "Wait!" I sometimes feel like shouting. "Take me back to 1977. Let me start again and do it all differently." But then sometimes I don't, even though I remember years when the sense of desperation was like an unwelcome visitor that kept showing up at my front door, demanding to be let in and against whom the door had to be barred. But I wasn't always unhappy, far from it. I was just not where I belonged, or where I thought I should be, and it sometimes struck with a force like panic. It's different now, of course, but I remember that sense. Reading Mary's letters, when she was feeling some of the same things, can bring it all back.

We live in an age where people travel for the purpose of being on the plane, being in the air between things. For what purpose? I often think, when I'm on yet another trans-Atlantic flight, of the weeks and months of my life that have been spent suspended in the ether, above the world, out of life and time. Every time I get on a plane, I feel the same old feeling. I'm twenty-five again and off to see the man I'm going to marry, or going to another country to take a job that will teach me—what? I've learned that experience isn't always completely useful. Sometimes it's just going through the motions because the motions are there to be gone through. But then lots of things in life are not invariably meaningful. Jobs, trips, parts of our education: many of them we could do without and be no worse off. The trick is turning any of it to good use. Write it down. Use it as fodder. Mary did. Everything became a story, and every story became part of who she was, or was becoming.

I think about Mary's life, crisscrossing the continent, never sure if she wanted to go or wanted to stay, drawn by so many conflicting calls. And it reminds me of my own life, back and forth across the ocean on the jumbo jets that have replaced the trains Mary took: so much easier, but so much less real. I'm in London on a September morning right now. If I really, really wanted to, or had to, I could be out of the door in half an hour; at the airport in two; and on a plane to San Francisco by noon. I could be walking up the steps of the house I grew up in in time for dinner. How strange it is to know we can, if we want, let go of one life that easily.

Homesickness: it's an ailment I've been familiar with for a long time. I left my much-loved California when I was twenty-one. I turned twenty-two in Oxford, twenty-three and twenty-four back in California, and I've never had a birthday in California since. Twenty-five and twenty-six happened in Spain, and since then it's always been England, a country in which I never dreamed I'd spend my life. But I have.

I suppose I might feel differently if I ever really let go of California. After all, lots of people move. But as it was for Mary, my ties were strong, and like Mary I had a close family to return to, always, and a place I loved. So the question was inevitable—why stay away?

Now I can come and go as I please. But leaving my adopted home would create new conundrums. Like for Mary, who once wrote, "I love my West when I am in the East," my nostalgia for England is profound when I am away.[36] When summer visits to California last more than a few weeks, I find myself reading English novels and thinking wistfully of Greenwich Park. And yet the sense of familiarity I have in California is compelling; the sense that one belongs in a particular place can be overwhelming. So again, I sometimes ask, Do I want to stay? (Yet writing in 2020, these decisions seem easier to make; one is older, the world is worse.)

Mary must have sometimes asked that question, especially when Arthur's business ventures failed so dismally in Idaho and his problems with alcohol became critical. She and Arthur might have led the sort of transcontinental life some of the people they knew did, like Arthur's sister and brother-in-law, Mary and James Hague, who were constantly crisscrossing the country. Early in their marriage there were periods when Arthur was away for months at a time, when Mary did go back to Milton, New York, and stayed at the family farm.

But the answer for Mary, if not easy, was clear. She loved Arthur and wanted to be with him. When things got really bad, late in the Idaho years, and she went away for a summer to Victoria, British Columbia, she wrote to Helena:

July 5, 1889
This experiment has settled one thing in my mind. There is no use my thinking I could go anywhere with the children for their improvement and my own away from my old boy. I'm irrevocably committed to the part of an anxious wife.[37]

However, when she got back to Idaho in August, she found that Arthur had been on a tremendous bender, and on August 8 wrote a doleful letter to Helena, which she later regretted.

August 25, 1889
Dearest Helena
I wrote you a dreadful letter—when was it, ago? Since then all has gone so differently, that I must ease your heart with regard to me. Even though the times of rest may not last forever, they are still times of rest; and you must think of me now as in smooth water for the present.[38]

Whether this was entirely true or not, it was important to Mary that Helena thought it was. But one wonders if Helena received such letters with trepidation; it was quite a responsibility to be Mary's main sounding board. Clearly Mary was aware of this also, and her next letter reveals her uneasiness that she may have gone too far in her previous letter:

September 15, 1889
Perhaps there will be a letter from you soon. I am always scared at a silence on your part, following an outburst of mine. For I never can remember quite what I have said, nor can calculate its effect at a distance, and on paper. Simply I must never allow myself to breakout on paper! It is altogether useless and misleading—[39]

But there is no indication of a reply until October 25, when Mary wrote to Helena, addressing her as "My dearest of Friends," saying that a letter from her always "booms up" her day. Something had been received from Helena, at long last.

One thing is certain; Mary's letters to Helena were not just correspondence. It was essential to Mary's well-being to be *heard* by someone she thought understood her and helped her retain a connection to her previous life and self.

The historian Rodman Paul, the editor of *A Victorian Gentlewoman in the Far West,* Mary's reminiscences, wrote in another publication:

> Here is a lady who spent years praising the beauties of the west, while wishing she were among her relatives and friends in the east. Intellectually and aesthetically she loved the west, but emotionally she loved the east.[40]

I think this aptly sums up the nature of the conundrum felt by the exile. One misses the old place, but knows one will miss the new place if one goes back. Is there an answer? Perhaps only in the drama of nature. Certainly, nature provided a kind of answer for Mary.

Mary's old world had had dramatic nature in it—perhaps not Sierras and waterfalls or endless deserts, but a natural world that had its own mystery and beauty. This is the description of the woods near her family's farm in Milton, New York, taken from her memoirs:

> The lane past the Mill House went up between old pastures to the Long Pond woods and that was our road to Arcady. That way we went for the first wild flowers in spring and the first skating in winter; we took our visitors up there, when we were girls, to stroll in the June moonlight—the young poets and artists of those lyric summers when sonnets were born overnight like the roses in the garden. You turned off from the hedgerows perfumed with wild grape blossoms that lined the lane, crossed the upper dam by one of those old foot-paths hid in willows, and directly you were in the perfect woods. And through them you came to Old Pond, mysterious and lonely. You never met anyone and you could not hear the mill. It was "the dreadful hollow behind the little wood" to me at the age when I first read Tennyson—but I have read him at all ages.[41]

This description has little in common with the strange and new sights Mary saw in the West. Rather, it reveals the sense of belonging in a world utterly familiar. This is a landscape that revealed to a young

Mary the mystery and beauty in her own life. How then did the grand vistas of the West reveal the innermost recesses of her soul? Mary had read Emerson. The great thinker's precepts in *Nature* resonated clearly for her:

> 1. Words are signs of natural facts.
> 2. Particular natural facts are symbols of particular spiritual facts.
> 3. Nature is the symbol of spirit.[42]

If Mary sees Nature as a symbol of the spirit, what kind of change is she going through as she embraces the western landscape? There is a passage in the reminiscences in which she describes once again traveling across the high plains of Idaho, many years after they had left behind the ruins of their great hopes there when Arthur's visionary irrigation scheme failed:

> But even now, on our continental journeys, when we have reached that country of the high valleys and the old lava-flows between the knees of the ranges; when we halt at some lone junction or water-tank in the sage brush and step out to breathe that air again and listen to the "essential silence" after the roar of the train—it is there, that whisper of the desert wind—it all comes back, the shiver of an old longing and doubt and expectancy.... We see the long low house stretched out on the Mesa raised above the valley, we see the ring of mountains lifting and lowering down to the great gate where the sun is setting in a storm of gold. The purple shadows darken in their canons; the color mounts to the zenith and the plains are flushed with light.[43]

Perhaps self-consciously, Mary refers to what comes back to her in the "essential silence" in terms of ambition—the house, the irrigation scheme—but I think this is disingenuous. Mary knew she was writing for a public (this, after all, is in her memoirs) attuned to themes of western grandeur and achievement. What she is talking about here is that overwhelming sense of presence one feels in nature: that "place where words stop," as Sharon Butala describes the sense of being in the presence of the very real but wholly inexplicable, which is the numinosity of pure nature itself.[44] Mary is talking about something most of us have known if we are lucky, that inexpressible sense of *being* in a place and feeling its presence wash through us. The transcendentalists tried to explain it; Muir got closer in his descriptions of the West; but Mary expresses it in language that in its immediacy and with its artist's imagery goes to the heart of an experience that evades expression. It is revealed more often in poetry than in prose, but Mary's prose captures it.

Mary's acknowledgment of the sublime nature of what she sees is far more than simple vision: she is in the landscape; her oneness with the soul of the land is indisputable. In the following she writes of Kuna, a spot that if you visited today, as I did a few years ago, you might see nothing. Mary might have seen nothing. But just listen to what she wrote:

> No one remembers Kuna. It was a place where silence closed about you after the bustle of the train, where a soft, dry wind from great distances hummed through telegraph-wires and a stage road went out of sight in one direction and a new railroad track in another; but that wind had magic in it. It came across immense dry areas without an object to harp upon except the man-made wires. There was not a tree in sight—miles and miles of pallid sage-brush: as moonlight unto sunlight is that desert sage to other greens. It gives a great intensity to the blue of the sky and to the deeper blue of the mountains lifting their snow-capped peaks, the high light along the far horizon.[45]

How can one ever look at sagebrush again without the thought that, "as moonlight is to sunlight is that desert sage to other greens," and understanding not only the contrast of color but the contrast of essential being? The experience is almost synesthetic: one can understand the nature of the life she is describing through this most perfect metaphor.

I have been to Kuna and have stood where that train platform once did. True, there are trees now—not many, and not grand nor very tall, but a few. It was a wet and dull day when I stood there, trying to imagine what Mary saw and felt. But in the end, I admitted failure. Mary had a vision and an eye for detail not given to many. It was a gift.

Some of Mary's descriptions, while effective, do not reach similar heights, though their warmth personalizes and makes accessible through familiar motifs a landscape otherwise alien to her readership. Consider the closing of her early novel *John Bodewin's Testimony:*

> Wind of the great Far West, soft, electric, and strong, blowing up through gates of the great mountain ranges, over miles of dry savannah, where its playmates are the roving bands of wild horses, and the dust of the trails which it weaves into spiral clouds and carries like banners before it! Wind of prophecy and hope, of tireless energy and desire that life shall not satisfy. Who that has heard its call in the desert, or its whisper in the mountain valleys, can resist the longing to follow, to prove the hope, to test the prophecy.[46]

The prose here leans toward purple, with its banners and prophecy, its callings in the desert, whispers in the valleys; and yet the personified wind, "soft, electric, and strong, blowing . . . over miles of dry savannah," saves this passage from fulsomeness. The electricity of the wind is something Mary felt in her soul. Her novels may have been written to make money, but as this passage shows us, there is some utterly luminous prose in even the most humble of them.

Understanding Exile

In the ancient world, exile was the worst that could happen, a fate more terrible than death. Exile has carried the stigma of punishment for heinous disgrace for centuries. Yi-Fu Tuan states: "The links binding a person to his hearth, to the family domain, and to his city were of a religious nature. . . . No bond could be more important; to break it was an act of impiety."[47]

It was perhaps partly this sense of her western life not being *right* in some very atavistic sense that augmented Mary's vexed relationship with the West; despite her deep appreciation of the landscape, it was not "home." She missed that indescribable sense of *rightness* that Tuan alludes to, and which one recognizes when one is in the familiar landscapes of childhood. The strangeness of the western landscape, although often sublime, had no eastern equivalents, or at least no equivalents in Mary's own life. And yet she was happy a lot of the time. She learned to be happy despite the fact that she felt herself to be out of the world in which she truly belonged. Mary's New York had been a vital place, full of events, thinkers, people of all persuasions—even in that simpler time. The natural world of Milton, and the family and farm, were important to her too, but it was culture and cultivated people that had attracted her most in her young days in the city.

It's interesting to hear Mary's comments on others who also considered themselves foreign to the place they were in. When she was spending the summer in Victoria, British Columbia, in 1889, she wrote to Helena, revealingly:

> May 26, 1889
> The town is very suburban and so are the people—most of them "hark back" in their sentiments and talks to England, and are anxious to explain that Victoria does not represent them; just as we Eastern women in the West talk. I am very lonely; and as often I could cry as laugh at these peculiarities of the exile, that I know so well.[48]

This very interesting comment reveals Mary's self-knowledge and also reveals the complexity of her situation. She appreciates the fact that "exiles" often over-explain themselves, falling into "peculiarities." But the way out of this situation is not obvious to her, nor to any of us who find ourselves in similar situations. One recognizes those "peculiarities." Every nationality becomes more itself, sometimes to the point of absurdity, when it feels under threat either ideologically or culturally.

Mary's self-knowledge gave her an eye for those who, like her, didn't belong. I'm thinking of one of her unusual pictures, *The Girl of the Mexican Camp,* which appeared in *Scribner's* in 1878. In it, the face of a Mexican girl, probably thirteen or fourteen, looks out at the reader with an intensity that is both arresting and disturbing. That face, nearly a century and a half old, looks as if it were drawn yesterday. I wonder what Mary felt drawing that picture: that they were worlds apart, or that they were a bit too close for her liking?

I'm not sure I can read the expression of the girl in the picture, but it reminds me very much of the famous cover of the June 1985 issue of *National Geographic,* a portrait of an Afghan refugee girl with piercing green eyes, Sharbat Gula, photographed by Steve McCurry. But Mary's picture was a drawing. She had to see into those eyes to capture them the way she did. I don't see anything like this in any other nineteenth-century drawing in *Scribner's*. Many of Mary's drawings have that same quality of immediacy, currency. She was reticent; she didn't talk too much about her feelings—except to Helena—but she understood things, as this very telling drawing reveals. One's own difficulties in life almost inevitably give one insight into the lives of others. Mary hadn't been through a lot by the time she drew this picture—her significant western trials were to come—but she saw something in this girl's eyes that she recognized, that recognized her. It's a slightly disturbing picture, unlike almost anything else of hers I can think of. I can imagine the scenario:

"Arthur, I'm going to go down to the Mexican camp this morning to draw one of the children there, if I can find her, the water-carrier's daughter. She has the most extraordinary face. Richard wants more illustrations for the piece on the California mining camp."

"Take Stranger with thee. And give the father a dollar."

"I'd rather give it to the daughter."

"He would only take it from her. Give her fifty cents. He may let her keep that."

. . .

They stare at me, but not in any way I am afraid of. There they are. His family. The water-carrier. Ah yes. Here he comes.

. . .

It wasn't too difficult to make them understand. I'm sure they won't take the money unless I force it on them. Perhaps I'll just leave it on the chair they have brought me. Here comes the girl.

"Buenos días, señora."

"Buenos días hija mia."

It sounds so strange to call her "my daughter," but I've heard them say it. And she's smiling, so it must be right. Can I make her understand how to sit and look into the distance, with the blanket slightly round her face, as if she were cold? She's smiling again. Am I making her feel ridiculous? Or am I the one who is ridiculous? There. If she will lean against the wall and wrap the blanket round her as though it's not seventy-five degrees outside! Richard wants illustrations for the piece. Now if she will sit still. Of course she will. She's not an energetic American girl. They've been taught to sit still. Not to expect much. What different worlds we come from. Does she feel it? I wonder if she despises being asked to be "picturesque"?

Oh, here comes Mama with a glass of water. I hope the glass is clean. Not one for the girl?

"Gracias, señora."

She's going to stay and watch. I'll do a copy of it for her. She probably has never had a picture of her daughter. The daughter has probably never seen or imagined herself this way.

They are kind. But their lives, so different. So different even from working people in Milton. And the women. So confined. The girl looks like she knows that. I wonder if she resents me? I'm probably twelve or thirteen years older than her. She's about fifteen or sixteen. Sixteen, the age I was when I was planning to move to New York to go to Cooper. What a different world. What will she do, this Mexican beauty? Marry one of the boys who work in the mine, or tends the horses at the hacienda? Have five or six children who will grow up quickly and do the same? Can she read? Can she write?

. . .

There. Finished. And the copy. It won't take long.

"Si, señora. Es para usted."

Now if I can give the daughter the dollar. She is saying no, but I am going to give it to her. There. I pressed it into her hand and felt her thin bones, like the bones of a bird. She looked away. Did I make her feel ashamed? I hope not. She needs the money. The father is nowhere around. Good. She can have it.

"Adios. Gracias."

. . .

"Here comes the water-carrier, Arthur. I wonder what for?"

"He came to say thank you for the picture. And his wife has sent us a present."

"Tortillas."

"Fresh from the oven. Have one. They'll be delicious."

That's how I'd imagine it. Mary didn't write about every experience she had, but there had to be some like that. Because they don't figure in her letters, it seems that she didn't have much to do with the working people. But they do figure in her fiction and in her drawings. It was perhaps that she felt them beneath Helena's interest, Helena who was friends with presidents, poets, and painters; Mary, who knew the water-carrier's daughter.

Such experiences must have made a sensitive thinker like Mary consider the fact that we are all exiles from somewhere, or are descended from those who were. But perhaps I'm giving a twenty-first-century understanding to a nineteenth-century woman. Perhaps Mary didn't see or feel that. Yet the picture *The Girl of the Mexican Camp* suggests a sympathetic understanding and fellow feeling that is not feigned.

Reflections on Transformation—An Interpretation

I see a woman sitting at a desk. She's not young, but still animated and alive: she sees things in the distance with her mind's eye. She's writing a memoir right now, remembering her life as an exile. She's had quite a life. She changed her life completely for a man, and lived with it even when it seemed like a mistake. She made the best of it and ended up with so much: a life full of events and love, and a knowledge of the world—the real world that is under our feet. That's not to say she would not have had those things anyway if she'd stayed at home. But it would have been different. She had the life she chose. That's Mary's life. But it's my life too.

A woman sits at her desk. 1922. She is writing. I am sitting at my desk, typing. 2020. We are trying to do the same thing: tell the story of our lives.

Hers. Where to begin?

1873. There's a doorway, and through it walks a man. You are sitting, knees up, drawing in a sketchbook. The young man enters this high-shelved, paneled room in a house where you are both visitors. You act startled, but you're not. He acts apologetic, but he's not. He followed you here, and you know it and are glad. The party was dull. You disappeared here to be with yourself and do something worthwhile. When you were gone, he saw no one, no one at all. The room became a desert; so, breaking all laws of propriety, he came; he walked down the long hallway and guessed that the library was where you would be. And of course, you were.

Fifteen years pass. You aren't so young anymore, but neither is he. You've got three children and are a world away from that library. He's a mining engineer. You've made a living illustrating, and now writing novels. There's another doorway. I'm looking at it from here, a century and more away, and I see it open and you come out into the air. Behind you is your house, the stone house he built you there in Boise Canyon. The two older children are in their schoolroom with the English woman who has come all this way out of love and loyalty to your family—she's the daughter of one of your old teachers at the Cooper Union School of

Design, in New York—to teach your children. Cooper Union: Sometime later they'll throw you a lifeline and ask you to be principal—after years out of the swing of the sea—and you'll refuse. From what? Pride? Fear? No, love, for the man, of course, but also for the places: the western places that took your youth and gave nothing back but themselves. And this high, wide, open, grassy desert: it made demands; it took without giving back. And still you loved it. And of course, it did give back, in ways you understand but can't explain.

Another woman is holding the new baby. You do have help, Mary, out here in the wilds of Idaho. And why not? Arthur would not expect you to live any other way. You draw. You write. You keep the family afloat with your work when Arthur's ventures are lost on the turbulent sea that is the West in which you live.

You've come out of the doorway, leaving your stone house in the canyon behind, and you walk out into the air. The wild grass is knee-high, dry and pungent. It's summer. The dry, hot wind is blowing. You need air. You've been writing all morning. You breathe it in. It's warm but not impossibly hot today, and you are glad to be outside. You always are. You were a farm girl, after all, a lifetime ago in Milton, New York, before you went to the city and became one of the best known young illustrators of your time, spending your days with the "most brilliant and fascinating young people of their time," as you said yourself, before you left it all and plunged into your life. Leapt into your life, for it was a leap of faith. And you never broke faith, even when faith broke with you. You walk up the hill behind the house, turning for a moment to wave at the young woman holding your baby. The baby looks up a moment, then turns, blinking, away from the brightness, and they go back inside.

You're not going anywhere, just clearing your mind. Walking. The pace steadies your thoughts and you feel your steps in time with your heart, beating. You hear your breath as the path gets steeper and you step out to get to the top of the hill, just to get the view.

You're up there now. You turn, north, south, east, west. You can see the world, blown into life. This wind. You think about it. It's got life of its own. Sometimes it's terrible, but days like this you don't mind it, blowing away the heat. It's full of light and heat and movement, and what? Full of itself in a way you understand but can't explain. Arthur understands. You might tell him about it. But you really don't talk about things like that. Not much. This way of seeing, of feeling, it's not something for words. You can draw it. It's your life, your life now. You're not longing for the old life, you're living the new life, the new world, in all its unimaginable antiquity. It pours through you. And it pours through me as I see you. It's 130 years ago, and you are walking up those hills. You live there because of your husband's work. But you are truly present in the landscape. Life is difficult, but you do more than bear it: you are alive to everything around you. You experience it and give it back in your drawing and writing, the good and the bad.

Mine:

I cycle up a street in London. It's October, but milder than it ought to be. Global warming. I smell coal smoke and think of how I first smelled it years ago, when we lived in a village in the country. Exotic to a Californian: that oh so evocative scent of winter in northern places. The light has got that perfect autumnal cast you sometimes see here—it only lasts an hour or so this time of year: slightly pink, cool and clear. The sunlight coming at its autumn angle tells me something is different. It's so far north here, so the light comes in a way I never saw when I was growing up in that long-ago time in California. There the light was vivid, yellow and warm, even in November. Fall came, of course, but it didn't speak in these delicate tones. I know that many people don't feel this way about places. Not everyone was brought up watching the changes in a landscape as familiar as one's own face.

I grew up in a small town, but a town that was close to the larger world. I would sit for hours on the roof of the house—conveniently reached by a small doorway onto a flat roof that gave onto twin peaks. What child would not have climbed up there? From the top of the house I could see for miles in every direction. Mount Tamalpais, Mount Diablo, the North Bay. It was magic for a young person to have that kind of perspective. So even if I didn't go places, I saw places. It was my own private mountaintop. And from that mountaintop I thought I could see the future. But I never imagined England. I think I hoped for something like Santa Cruz, or the hills of Marin County. Europe? Maybe Paris or Italy. But I knew nothing. England didn't speak to me. In some moods I thought of it and saw Dickens's orphans and Jane Eyre's attic and shuddered. And part of me still shudders, even in hip, multicultural London. Sometimes the atmosphere of the city still feels like it's caught somewhere in the past, but not my past. It sometimes still feels like the place I came to, aged twenty-one, the fall of 1977. California in 1977 seemed cool and forward looking. Now it all seems different. Had I stayed I'd have understood those changes, but my vision of it is frozen, preserved in the amber that is one's personal history—the light of the past shining through like colors in a stained-glass window, illuminating, beautifying, and distorting.

That happened to Mary too. She writes about it. She says she opened drawers where clothes that had lived the other life were packed away, and by their scent alone she was overcome with that sense of loss that the exile knows so well.

It was this that drew me to her, immediately: that sense that she, too, knew what this thing was, this life in two places, this identity that is never quite fixed. Am I English? Am I American? Was Mary a westerner? Was she an easterner who just lived in the West? There are a lot of us now, hybrids: born one place, living somewhere not just different but *other.* There was little in my American life that prepared me to become the person I am now (except a voracious and extensive reading habit that taught me all I know about most of the places I'll never go). And that is part of the life of the exile: transformation.

Transformation

Mary's western transformation gave her a perspective she might not have acquired in New York, where, if she had not met Arthur Foote, she would have undoubtedly stayed. Going west in 1876 gave her a new template, a new vision of the world. It might be argued that it was mainly Mary's western experience that was transformative and resulted in her appreciation of a new and foreign landscape. I think that while experience undoubtedly affected her, it was also her early formation as an artist, and as a Quaker, as well as her innate sensitivity and awareness, that gave her the capacity to embrace a world in which all the landmarks were new ones and many of the natural signs had new meanings. It was not simply that the unwritten land became the space on which her artist's soul inscribed meaning, but rather that the meaning inherent in the land, its own reality, written in its own being, was accessible to Mary because of her deep respect for, sensitivity to, and openness to nature, in ways both literary and artistic. She took to the West the tools she needed to address its multifaceted complexity and many contradictions. In an essay on Mary and her work, Shelley Armitage expresses this point perfectly:

> The heart of her writings remains . . . firmly grounded in the perception of the artist's eye. The resulting conception is an effort to dramatize the tension between the poetic and the actual. Mrs. Foote's ability to externalize the subliterary experiences of the West hinged on her sensitivity and technique as an illustrator. The result is an authenticity in her fiction generated by the perception and depiction of a mythical West other than that popularized by mainstream western critics and authors—an inner reality with all its attendant ambiguities.[49]

This "inner reality" was very much a female reality, depicting the West as a realm of female endeavor, not just the male heroism so often depicted by male artists. Equally, Mary's fiction—written from that most female of impulses, keeping the family financially stable while the husband tried his hand at different strategies—is the literature of female protagonists in difficult western situations. Mary Hallock Foote was the first female artist of stature whose main subject was the West. She was also arguably the first significant novelist who wrote about the West from a feminine perspective.

It is for this reason that I find a rather arch comment made by the respected critic Nina Baym slightly exasperating. In her brief mention of Mary in her book on western women writers, she states, "Each novel has its obligatory love story, but Foote is more interested in men's than women's work."[50] It is not so much that Mary was not interested in woman's work, but that she did not regard women's work as purely domestic in itself. She was a professional woman, an accomplished, productive artist, brought up with a Quaker sense of gender equality, and had a supportive husband who did not believe that it was necessary that his wife also be his servant. Nonetheless, Mary was a devoted wife and mother, and her labors for her family, while they might not have included the most physically grueling and tedious—for that she had help, just as Arthur would not have dug the mines he surveyed—were unending. From her feminine perspective it is not necessary to be solely rooted in domesticity to be female, which is what Baym's remark seems to suggest. Western stories were frequently "men's stories." Women who wanted to read about the West were often "resisting readers" of stories in which female concerns were absent or solely domestic.[51] After all, the first popular literature by and for women in

America was the captivity narrative, the popular tales of women being abducted by hostile natives. While the captors had changed, one often gets the sense that in the West women were "captives" of a particularly arduous sort of domestic life. Certainly, life was very tough for a large number of women, but men's labors somehow took on the mythic status of the cowboy-knight errant, at least in popular culture, whereas women remained "in the kitchen" for the most part, and were therefore not considered the subject matter of romantic speculation, except insofar as they crossed into men's narrative, or were actually made captive and in need of rescue.

Mary Hallock Foote was in the vanguard of writers who talked about women who were neither victims nor tied to purely domestic situations. This reveals a deep ambiguity at the root of the perception of a woman's role in the West; that is, were women able to embrace western freedom, as the putative western hero did, or was her role that of an adjunct to that same man? Mary's fiction deals with this ambiguity, and adds the complicating factors of East versus West, as well as the problems attendant on the assumed feminine desire for stability, particularly when children are involved, as opposed to the ever-optimistic, ever-wandering man on the frontier. In Mary's letters we hear these questions asked at their most personal level. The following relatively cheerful observation, written from Santa Cruz where Arthur was trying to develop a formula for cement and where the family's livelihood was rather precarious, is typical:

> October 29, 1877
> Things are quite exciting with us—Santa Cruz or the wide wide world—Cement and a home for a few years or at least 'till we go home to the dear "old country"—or Mining Camps and howling wildernesses. The latter are splendid fun when there is no baby—but you can imagine how one feels about a teething child however healthy and no decent doctor.[52]

Even though her domestic concerns did loom large, Mary still saw the West with a keen artist's eye, and she felt it with a lover's heart and was often enraptured by the beauty with which she was surrounded. Rapture, for a gently bred Victorian Quaker lady, was not something publicly displayed. Even in Mary's letters there is reticence in personal matters. Therefore, like other intimate revelations, her most profound feelings about the natural world of the West do not appear in her novels, memoirs, and sketches, except obliquely. It is only in her letters to her most trusted friend, Helena, that Mary revealed her deeply felt thoughts concerning the natural world.

Compared with the commentaries that accompany her lovely drawings in the 1889 series that appeared in *Century,* Pictures of the Far West, Mary's epistolary descriptions of her actual environment are rich and human. By contrast her journalism was written for a known audience, one for whom the expectation was for a familiar, if somewhat overwrought, descriptive style. The following example from "The Irrigating Ditch," which appeared in the June 1889 issue of *Century,* is a case in point:

> West of the Missouri there are immense, sad provinces devoted to drought. They lie beneath skies that are pitilessly clear. The great snow-fields, the treasury of waters, are far away, and the streams which should convey the treasure are often many days' journeys apart. These wild water-courses are Nature's commissaries sent from the mountains to the relief of the plains; but they scamper like pickpockets. They make away with the stores they were charged to distribute. They hurry along, making the only sound to be heard in those lands which they have defrauded. Year by year, or century by century, they plow out their barren channels: gradually they sink, beyond any possibility of fulfilling their mission. Now and then one will dig for itself a grave in the desert, bury its mouth in the sand, and be known as a "lost" river.[53]

Lost rivers! She might as well say "lost souls," so freighted with heavy symbolism is this passage, likening a natural phenomenon to the Miltonic journey of a soul from Paradise to damnation. The nineteenth century liked this kind of fulsome eloquence, with its great crescendos of oratorical opulence. One can almost see the speaker shaking her head in dismay before launching into the corollary, "Meantime the long-repressed soil vents itself in extravagant, contorted growths of sagebrush."[54] My point is that in her public writing Mary Hallock Foote presented the accepted face of the western landscape. She wrote for a public that wanted its imagery grand and profound, drenched in worthy moralizing and Bierstadtian vistas—one might say a male voice, for journalism was predominantly male.

Interestingly, however, the illustration that accompanies this particular piece of mildly verbose prose is quite different: a wistful mother stands at the side of the irrigation ditch, holding an infant who struggles in her arms. The mother's long-suffering face retains its placidity as she observes water flowing through the open sluice gate. In the distance, we can make out the shadowy form of her husband, presumably the bringer of this bounty, laboring at some task. Newly sprung vegetation lines the ditch, spindly trees and long grasses. The woman's look conveys neither relief nor undue satisfaction; she observes, as if reserving judgment, passive and resigned, awaiting the results of her partner's endeavors. (One wonders if there's a hidden subtext here, considering Arthur's troubled Idaho irrigation scheme, an ambitious, even visionary plan that failed due to the repeated breakdowns in funding.)

What a difference from either of these options we find in Mary's own letters:

> December 16, 1887
> I long to burst out once in a while and tell you how proud I am of this really great work. It is *making a country* as large as a small state—and if in its isolation and virgin barrenness it is so poetic a land—what will it be with long lines of gleaming ditches traversing its vast levels with fields of alfalfa and herds of cattle, and rows of poplars marking the boundaries of the farms. But I know what fatuity it must seem to you. It is the fate of a scheme to be classed with all other forms of idiocy until it has proved itself a success—So I will hold in. We are not broad here, like the landscape, but very intense; and we worship our common dream, for which each in his or her own way, has sacrificed something.[55]

One hears the true voice, full of power, life, and intensity, a voice that embraces the labor and sacrifice required to fulfill this unpoetic but grand plan. This is not just the artist or author's voice; this is the personal voice, deeply invested in the success of her husband's irrigation scheme, and aware of the integrity of the landscape itself; and aware, too, of the significance of having sacrificed for a dream. The sacrifice invests the dream, and hence the landscape, with a sacramental import,

The Irrigating Ditch, Century, June 1889.

appropriately, since the dream is "worshipped." This brings us back to the point that Mary's knowledge of the landscape, and relationship to it, had something religious in its nature; her aliveness to the numinous qualities of the world around her not only establishes links with the transcendentalists but also reveals a deep personal connection with the spiritual presence inherent in nature.

Interpretation of Landscape

Mary's complex feelings about the western landscape are evident early on. In a letter written in November of 1876, shortly after she arrived in the West, she recounted some of her earlier observations about traveling westward.

> November 5, 1876
> When we crossed the great Laramie Plains there was a sunset which I shall always remember—the sun dipped below the vast line where sky and plain met—there it seemed to wait and eye us with a strange dull glare. It could only have been a few minutes, but the impression was so strong that it made the vision seem to last any length of time, almost, and even after it was gone below the dim verge of the plain, I could still see it, looking with a red and fixed eye. The motion of the cars seemed to make it more still, and like a vision, as when the cars whirl you swiftly past a stream of rippling water, the ripples look as if carved, or painted in a picture.[56]

The extraordinary visual quality of this observation heightens the surreal nature of what she is actually seeing. This combination of movement and stillness give the scene a quality of threatening wonder. Later when she had become accustomed to the California landscape, she wrote:

> September 14, 1876
> Day after day there is the same unvarying brightness and calm—It is beautiful—for a long time it is wonderfully exhilarating but there comes a time when it makes one desperate. The sunshine seems like a thing one is doomed to, instead of a blessing.[57]

This expresses the mixed feelings Mary had toward the new landscape in which she found herself, but also expresses the acknowledgment of its grandeur and *otherness*.

In the letter of September 14, a mention of being prisoners of the landscape obliquely suggests the early colonial narratives of female captivity and reinforces the ambiguity present in an otherwise unambiguous picture. Further examples in her letters reveal similar mixed reactions, yet a profoundly appreciative understanding, indeed sympathy, for her adopted land, particularly as her familiarity with it increased:

> The *patience* of this land during the long thirsty months is enough to break one's heart—and the way in which a smile of tender green slowly wanders over the sun-baked, cracked hopeless hills, after the rains—If I were a poet I should shed tears at the sight of grass

> springing from ground that looks as if it covered the entrance to that place where all who enter leave hope behind.[58]

When she wrote those words, Mary was barely seven months into a lifetime's western sojourn. She was twenty-nine years old, not yet a mother. Patience, calamity, and something near to despair were still ahead of her. Her life in the West would come near to breaking her heart, but her growing love for the landscape, even considering all the demands it made on her as a woman, a writer, and an artist, is clear.

> March 1877
> I thought I had grown too old to feel this stirring of the blood—that unreasonable, fitful, half tearful joy in the Spring—but it is here again—all the stronger perhaps for the strange influence of those long dry lurid months—I didn't know it affected me so much until it was all over.[59]

Mary was beginning to know the landscape like a friend. That she felt the way she did about a place that brought her so many disappointments testifies to both the power of the landscape and the depth of Mary's connection with the natural world. Unusually for the time, she writes of a landscape largely free of male domination. This is not to say there are not male influences in her writing. There are many, and many of her stories are firmly rooted in the masculine world of work, a world with which she was familiar through her husband's mining and irrigation work. But this is not my point. Rather, when I say her vision of landscape was largely free of male domination, I mean her view of the landscape of the West is not *mediated* through the male gaze, with which students of western literature are so familiar. She was not entirely alone in this. Janice Monk has written that Willa Cather and Mary Austin, two writers whom the reader of the West would almost certainly class with Mary,

> recorded views of the land that contrast with male interpretations. Cather's land can be brutal, but is beautiful and powerful, not submissive. Regeneration comes from the land, rather than from violence. Austin's land is feminine, but a strong woman, self-sufficient, forgiving, but unwilling to be molded by men's needs.[60]

Like Cather and Austin, Mary had a vision of the West that may have once been considered simply "local color" but reveals more than that not unworthy tradition. She did not collude with that tradition of the heroic sublime that fed so easily into the doctrine of Manifest Destiny. Rather she saw the landscape through both a naturalistic and female view. She did not look at landscape through the traditional western "virgin land" paradigm. In June 1887, Mary wrote a letter to Helena that was hardly romantic in its perception of the natural world:

> June 8, 1887
> Now in these later days, I believe I can see more clearly where I stand, or do *not* stand. The point of view of cultivation I can never have—but there is something terribly sobering about these solitudes, these waste places of the earth. They belittle everything one is, or tries to do.[61]

This is not the view of someone involved in the legacy of conquest, but rather someone who *meets* the landscape on its own terms and meets it with the respect it deserves. Nor is it Edmund Burke's sublime, that "delightful terror" so loved by the later Hudson River School of painters. Rather, this is a perception that takes in, understands the ambiguity and contrasts, and does not dramatize its object. Later in the same letter, she refers to

> the vast wonderful sunsets, the solemn moonlight—and the noise the river makes on dark nights. The waste of water and of land and the immense dignity of it all! Very few things in art hold their own against it.[62]

Art was the Claude glass through which a young Mary Hallock had seen the world.[63] To suggest that nature overtook art was a tremendous admission for the former star student of the Cooper Union School of Design, and one she would not have made before her western transformation. Her western pictures are neither sentimental nor romantic. When there is desolation, she draws desolation; when there is a domestic framing of the wilderness, we are given that. In their realism, her pictures give us an insight into the soul of the landscape that any number of sublime landscape paintings cannot.

Equally, in her novels and stories the plots are slightly contrived and the characters perhaps less developed than they might be, but nowhere is there a sense that the *landscape* has been painted in the colors expected by an eastern audience. She is true to her artist's vision in her role as a writer. This is most true in her letters, letters that were not subject to the demands of publishers or readers.

To briefly reiterate: Mary Hallock Foote's relationship with the natural world of the West was posited on both her formation as an artist and her innate sensitivity to the nuances of nature. Brought up in a farming community, and trained as an artist, she was already highly attuned to the rhythms of the agrarian world, the domesticated landscape, when she went west. This fine-tuning was manifested in observation: the artist's eye, the painter's stroke, the draughtsman's feeling for space and texture.

The world Mary Hallock Foote encountered in the West was not like the domesticated landscape of the East in which she had been raised. Rather, it was the unsettled West known by an eastern audience as a land of myth, misunderstanding, and fable. Her initial response to her new world was in some respects based on its contrast with "culture." Yet it was the contrast with domestic and cultivated landscape that most struck her, and efforts to domesticate western spaces were the subject of much of her art and fiction. Her affinity for natural beauty would certainly have made it easier for her to appreciate the western landscapes and to make them her own: to familiarize them, even; in her own terms, to domesticate them.

Domestication is something we do; when we find ourselves in a new environment, we make it our own, put our imprint on the place so that it loses its strangeness. In order for Mary Hallock Foote to be able to live in her new western landscape, she needed that landscape to be accessible to her deepest wells of feeling. I suggest that her response was *feminine* in the sense described by Janice Monk:

> Emergence of a sense of objectivity, or self as "other," characterizes male psychic development. This sense stems from the male's need to separate himself from the mother. By comparison, females, associating themselves with the mother, develop a psychic sense of

> fusion, empathy, and identification. Such theories have implications for the development of responses to nature and landscape as something which is object, detached from oneself, and manipulable, as opposed to responses that see nature and landscape as an extension of oneself to which one accommodates.[64]

In relation to Mary, this suggests that despite the initial strangeness of the western landscape, she was able to internalize the landscape, and identified with it in a way that transformed her perception and allowed her to understand the western landscape as few had done before her. This transformation contrasts with what many of her contemporaries did with their western perceptions, creating caricatures of the West in the shoot-em-up dime novels and pictures such as those created by Remington and Russell for a thrill-seeking eastern audience. Nothing could be further from Mary's understanding than that sort of popular imagery.

There is a kind of nature writing in Mary's canon that reaches "the place where words stop." Sharon Butala, whom I have quoted, refers to the understanding she gained of a landscape she began to know only in midlife. Both Butala and Mary have an understanding of nature that is distinctly spiritual. But Mary does not reveal this side of her knowledge of nature in her novels, her drawings, or her essays, except obliquely. The depth of her deeply felt, intuitive knowledge is revealed in her letters. This may seem like a long way round to suggest that Mary had an innate understanding of the natural world, but my point is that her view and understanding of the world of the West went beyond her training and experience. It was a deeply felt sense of the sublime, as well as an instinctive understanding of place that I would call absolutely feminine in the sense described previously, encompassing identification, fusion, and empathy. This understanding was expressed in her private correspondence rather than in her public persona and revealed the deep emotional connection she felt with land and landscape.

Consider a letter she wrote to Mary Austin in 1903 in which she praises that writer's perception and depiction of the desert landscape:

> October 12, 1903
> No-one can live in those lands of little rain without having moods that correspond to the nature that "hath us in thrall," a nature that

> is without mercy—in its unspeakable beauty and its power of awakening longing and unrest. Those times and seasons you least of all can hope to escape, but pray do not ever mistake those fallings off and "vanishings" for a sign of halting power; rather, I should interpret then as the power itself stormily stirring before it has found its best channel of expression through your searching and thrilling use of words. Only one of our great prose poets could write as you do of the un-writeable; tell as you can the un-tellable.... [It is] rich, unusual speech, straight of [*sic*] the mark, and a something besides that is pure woman.[65]

I find this "pure woman" comment particularly interesting, suggesting that Mary believes there is in female perception something different. In 1986, noted western scholar Melody Graulich wrote:

> Foote had a larger soul—and a larger experience—than she ever publicly voiced. In 1903 the 55-year-old author wrote a revealing letter to a new Western woman writer, Mary Austin, in which she praised Austin for writing of the West in a way "no one has done or is likely to do"; that is, writing the "unwritable" and telling the "untellable" in a style "that is pure woman." Foote was well aware of the difficulties of writing as a woman, and although she had created a West inhabited by women and emphasized their importance there, she knew that she had not dared to tell the untellable, that she had not given public expression to those "cries that one woman utters to another," possibly because she felt so cut off from a female audience. Her letters to Helena, unpublished, are her finest writing; there she wrote about the conflicts and difficulties of being a wife and mother in the West, about her art, ambitions, aspirations and emotional needs.[66]

This aspect of Foote's importance, her paving the way, as Graulich argues, for subsequent women writers who began to tell the story of the women's West, is essential to a full understanding of her importance. But as one who paved the way, Foote had many obstacles to overcome—not the least being her deeply felt sense of the absence of eastern culture and her longing for her family and friends there—despite the adventurousness of her western life. Consider Mary's comments in a letter to Helena:

> October 19, 1894
> Your lovely letters came to me at our camp at the "Thousand Springs"—a place Arthur has always wanted me to see since he first saw it when he was on the Irrigation Gov't work.... It was one of our beautiful trips. Boise, you know is just what we have to do, not at all what we wish to do. This took us into the only West which is to me "worthwhile"—not the social, "smart" West, but the West which will one day have its poets and its "cry."[67]

This letter seems quite chatty and ordinary until that final "cry." *Its cry:* this is the expression of the inexpressible, which Mary clearly felt. What a pity that she did not feel she could be the one to give the West its "cry." She was certainly capable. But as Melody Graulich suggests, her letters contain some of her finest writing and, I would add, her most deeply heartfelt. The following beautiful passage, which is in a letter from Santa Cruz, is an example of this kind of expressiveness:

> November 1877
> The rock is worn by the feet of fishermen climbing up & down. We sat there and looked at the dizzy rolling of the waves below—There were wild ducks & cormorants flying about—and a grand old gull sailed right over our heads. I looked up and saw how the edges of his feathers let the sunlight through like a gold fringe. He might have symbolized the Holy Spirit descending, only he had such a wide, restless sweep of his wings.[68]

This letter takes a more personal tone than we will find in Mary's fiction or her journalism, both of which were written for a reading public not attuned to the higher key that she allowed herself privately. Mary's illustration for the Santa Cruz piece titled "A Seaport on the Pacific," for the August 1878 issue of *Scribner's,* has some of the same qualities as her letter, dramatic yet intimate, and as ever her eye for detail is unmatched.

Another reason Mary was so in tune with the natural world was the she was actually *in* nature a great deal more than most women of her class. Consider her descriptions of a river adventure:

> August 19, 1884
> Well, my dear, it was a wild trip. The moonlight made it more difficult to distinguish between safe water and unsafe.... But I assure you it was wildly delightful. I was not a bit afraid.... There were places where even two women in the stern could know that we were in trouble—when the rapids were roaring in the middle of the river and the space of deep channel between them and the bluffs was very narrow and crooked besides.... We were two hours and a half going down, for the run is very winding. And beautiful beyond words, it was, to see those dream like shores pass us in the moonlight. It wasn't all rapids of course—There were long still reaches where we were carried along fast, but smoothly, but I confess there was something intoxicating in those little rushes past the rapids.[69]

This, I believe, is the kind of experience that Mary loved and lived for and accounts for a good deal of her love of the western landscape. Mary knew that she could not have had the adventurous life she did if she had stayed in the East. Yet part of her still longed for her old life.

However, the canyon in Idaho, where their lives were so intense and difficult, was the heart of Mary's western experience. Experience confirms that one returns in thought to the point of greatest intensity in life, where one felt most alive.

A comment in a letter from Mary to Helena, written from Grass Valley, California, Mary's final western home, after her daughter Agnes had suffered yet another bout of malaria, emphasizes this point: "So it goes: In Idaho we got rid of malaria and all our money (I speak as if we had *had* it!) but we had everything!"[70]

Although Mary was certainly happy in Grass Valley when they moved there, and far more comfortable in her living arrangements, she later frequently acknowledged that there was something in the life they led in the canyon in Idaho that had touched her soul and that she missed when they left it.[71] Shortly before they left Idaho for California, she wrote:

September 15, 1889
I rode up to the Canon the other day with Mr Tompkins, to make sketches for a Cañon story for St. Nicholas which I have just sent in.

We saw the house from afar off, seated on the hill, looking so like home that my heart fairly went out towards the spot. Little old Ed. trotted up the hill to give us welcome. Lollo knew his old corral—The piazza was all sunshine, but all silence, too. There was a single rose blooming on the bush under my bedroom window.

It was a hard experience in the time of it—yet the place was endearing—and if I could take the children there again for a summer, just as I went to Victoria, with a fixed income and all things settled it would be restful beyond anything—and then if Bessie would come too, with Birney!

It is a place that sets one dreaming—I fell at once under the old spell; only I could feel that the keen suspense had dropped away.[72]

The "old spell," the "magic" in the wind she writes of elsewhere; mountains compared to "the Holy Ones of old... meet[ing] their transfiguration"; these kinds of descriptions give us a clear insight into the view of the natural world of the West that Mary had. She glories in the sublime, the magnificent, but she also is alive to the land's own identity, its divinity, one might say, free of the interpretations we put on it and capable of affecting us as much as we may affect it.

Like John Muir's "heroic encounters with that beyond," as his transcendental experiences in nature have been described, Mary's experiences in nature more than once render her speechless, in that place where words stop and vision begins.[73] Early in her western life, she wrote of a "solemn radiant morning sky" and mountains that

> when all alight with color... seem to have a meaning with the shadow of some impending doom in it.... No matter how the wind may blow here... the light on the Mountains is always still as if they were part of another world." (Dec. 22, 1876)[74]

Are they part of another world—or that world that lies beyond the veil—Plato's reality behind the shadows? In this excerpt, and others like it, Mary reveals an openness toward the meanings in nature that are inexpressible: felt deeply but not spoken. And there are further references, if not to the divine then at least to the mythic, as here, when she described the South Park on the way to Leadville:

> May 12, 1879
> It seemed a playground for the Centaurs—so vast, so brilliant, so free and utterly unspoilable. There were the dark pine covered mountains and beyond the Snowy range—awful, beautiful, unreal![75]

It is the "unreality" here I would like to stress. "Unreal" is a commonly used adjective among us; not so in the nineteenth century. To describe a vista as unreal suggests a deep unknowableness about that particular prospect: a place beyond words. Again, we approach the sublime, but not in any conventional way. Mary's way into such experiences was, I believe, not cerebral but spiritual.

My point is this: I believe that Mary Hallock Foote had experiences of the natural world that partook of the spiritual, the sublime, the transcendental, the mystical. These epiphanic moments in nature are hinted at obliquely in her prose, but the prose was written with the reticence of the Victorian lady. She would have no more drawn on her intensely private experiences in nature than would she have written about her marriage, except in the broadest terms.

I return to Melody Graulich's description. Mary Hallock Foote had a "larger soul...than she ever publicly voiced." Her native reticence prevented her from revealing her deepest feelings to her reading public, except perhaps obliquely. But those feelings are revealed in her letters, and through them we may come to a better understanding of the rapture of her perception of the landscapes of the West.

What If?

There's a scene in *Angle of Repose* that might easily have happened. Susan (Mary), Augusta (Helena), and Thomas (Richard Gilder) are talking after dinner during one of Susan's visits back to New York. It's Thomas speaking:

> How art thou remarkable? Let me count the ways. Hmm? She's been out in the unhistoried vacuum of the West for nearly five years, as far from any cultivated center as possible. What does she

> do? She histories it, she arts it, she illuminates its rough society. With a house to keep and a child to rear, she does more and better work than most of us could do with all our free time. She goes to Mexico for two months and returns with a hundred magnificent drawings and what amounts to a short book—she writes as well as Cable and draws better than Moran. She has been over Mosquito Pass in a buckboard and across Mexico by stage coach and saddle horse, she has been down mines and among bandits, places where no lady ever was before, and been absolutely unspoiled by it. There isn't a roughened hair on her head. To cap it, she is so vivacious and charming that she makes an old political warhorse like Godkin beg for sugar lumps, and draws a hundred pairs of glasses to our box.[76]

It would be nice to think Mary got this kind of approbation. It's nice also that Stegner clearly recognized that Mary was indeed someone quite special, though giving her praise to the somewhat effete figure of Thomas somewhat lessens its impact. Nonetheless, it's a good summary of some of Mary's more remarkable achievements. And she was remarkable, though she wouldn't have ever considered herself so. And indeed, the age was full of people who lived remarkable lives, partly due to the fact that they were in remarkable places. But many people in the West did not lead lives of *appreciative understanding,* as Mary did. It would have been easy to fight against what one didn't immediately understand, and there is a bit of that in Mary's response to the West. The world of people came in for her criticism, the world of nature never. At one point, she writes to Helena that "it is the western *town* I weary of, so that I feel almost crazed with the pettiness and monotony; it is not the western country."[77] And that is exactly the point. One can imagine what the "unhistoried" West felt like to Mary, but the ancient landscapes, new to her eyes as if they had just been created, were entirely different. She saw the deep reality of nature in a way the nineteenth century often did not: she saw it with love and an understanding that approaches the mystical. What do I mean by mystical? I hear the reader asking. Just this: having an openness to the being of nature, an acceptance of the unknowability of it, and an identification of the self with that unknowable otherness. That was what Mary Hallock Foote did, quite as comprehensively as any more radical freethinker of her time, our time, or any time.

CHAPTER TWO

New Almaden

MARY'S WESTERN LIFE BEGAN in California, in Santa Clara County, where she had gone to join her young husband, Arthur, who was chief engineer of the New Almaden quicksilver (mercury) mine. Mary began writing about her new home as soon as she got there. The quality of Mary's western observations was remarkable from the beginning. When she got to California, she immediately began to frame her experience by drawing it, describing it in letters, and exploring her new world—this while completing a commission for the illustrations for *The Scarlet Letter,* beginning her married life, and becoming pregnant almost immediately. Here she writes to Helena, who has lost a child to one of the many illnesses that plagued them.

> October 4, 1876
> Shall I still keep telling you all about our life here? Does it really interest you? I would write volumes if I thought they would make one hour pass more easily to you. We have passed into a new phase of the climate—the transition from summer to winter. Morning and evening, we are wrapped in fog, that blows in wildly from the sea—fills the valley, and rises till we are muffled in its chill whiteness, I walk every morning after breakfast and it is so strange since the fogs came. I seem to be the only person in the whole world—I cannot describe to you the strange feeling it gives me to walk in this veiled landscape. It is so high up—I pass along the edge of steep ravines and know that on ahead where the road passes out of sight round a bend of the mountain lies a great stretch of valley & mountain below—but it is all a blank white cloud everywhere—only my insignificant self walking along in the perfect stillness. It is always very still here, (except just in the Camps, where children are playing in the streets) and the fog seems to deaden what little sound there usually is.[1]

I can see her walking through those California hills, her dog at her side. I have walked some of those same paths at New Almaden—it's a state park now—and I hope I have walked in Mary's footsteps once or twice. I know this landscape, and I can see and feel what Mary is describing. Walking in the "veiled landscape": yes, I know what you mean, Mary. It is a curious feeling. One disappears into the view, and the solitude, the quiet. The elemental stillness goes right to the heart. It's different from those vistas she experienced later in Leadville and Idaho. I wonder if Grass Valley brought it back—the Californian misty morning epiphany? It's like nowhere else.

Here she is, sketchbook in hand, starting out. She goes up and round the top of the hill behind the mine, where on a clear day you can see all the way to the San Francisco Bay. But it's foggy and misty today. Her dog, Stranger, growls at a noise, but it's only a squirrel or some other small animal. What is she thinking of as she walks those paths in summer and fall and early winter in 1876—she, becalmed in the West—while the rest of the world was turning? What was going on in the outside world was as far away as it could be, so she was thrown onto her own resources—of which she had many—and devices. Maybe she was thinking something like this:

I wonder what that flower is? I've never seen anything like it before. I wonder what Helena would think of this? Me in the woods of California, with this huge dog, and not a soul around. And the smells.... Hardly any birds—maybe I'm disturbing them.... But the quiet! It almost seems that the mountain is sleeping. Sleeping and breathing. It's so still, but so alive. I'm going to stop and draw this view. Has anyone ever drawn this? Has anyone even really seen it? Is a thing real if it's never been seen? Am I real, if no one knows me, and no one sees me? I feel like my old life was a dream, and that the only thing that is real is what I'm going through now. Is that true? Is that what life is? I'm so alone, but I'm within this new world. What does it have to tell me? What if Mother or Father or Bessie or Helena were to walk out from that turning in the path. Ha ha! How strange to imagine them here. And yet I almost feel like they are here, that I can see them. If I squint my eyes...But no, I can't think about it. I am here. Arthur is at the mine. Here is my dog...And the stillness. The quiet is almost speaking to me. Now the mist is lifting off that hilltop, the blue, blue sky looking down, like it knows me—but such a different blue from the sky at Milton, such a dry, crystal blue that goes on and on and on. This stillness, this knowledge that I am here, in this world, so small a part of it, and yet in it, what does it mean? What am I in this place? Am I moving, or is the world moving around me?

Perhaps we have more language for these experiences now—not that that makes them more real. Perhaps less so—yes, almost definitely less so. Mary's understanding of the self in nature is eloquent in its simplicity, not aided by a thousand muddy explanations. Her age did have a habit of extravagant prose—Mary falls into that herself at times. But her Quaker habit of stillness speaks more fluently in its reticence and silence, and in its metaphors, than any explanation or imagining of mine can.

Echoes of Ancient Greece

Years later, composing her memoirs, Mary looked back at the time in New Almaden. She wrote:

> We have worn out many a dry season since our first housekeeping began on that sun-baked hillside at New Almaden. I have grown used to them and learned to find a sort of content in their smiling, inscrutable, monotony; and the overpowering light and emptiness of the sky by day is marvelously atoned for by the nights—the great nights of stars.[2]

The contentment she finds in the "smiling, inscrutable, monotony" of the endless sunny days is something anyone who has lived outdoors in the heat of an inland Californian summer will know: those afternoon hours when the sun's relentless slow march across the sky feels like the sound of a hammer on iron, echoing in the dry, harsh air.

But this is afternoon stillness; it does not speak like a morning stillness—when "dawn with her fingertips of rose" touches the misty mountaintops. Homer said that of Greece, but it's true of Mary's California landscape as well. In fact, a lot of Mary's writing about the landscape reads like Homer. The transcendentalists were influenced by Homer, and Mary was influenced by them, so there's ancient Greece at two removes.

She says the days are "atoned for by the nights"—those starry western nights. Even before the Greeks, the sky was an object of awe and worship. Mary's regard for the starry nights has something of that same veneration, that speechless awe we feel but cannot explain in the presence of the vast wonder that we live with daily and hardly ever *see.*

It's not surprising that Homer echoes in Mary's writing. She lived most of her life in an arid country where dependence on a sometimes inscrutable and harsh natural world was a given, like in Greece. In a life lived intimately in nature, an appreciation and reverence for it is inevitable, as is a relationship that makes it familiar in all its moods. Like Mary Austin in the even harsher southlands, Mary Hallock Foote was later able to see beauty in places that less sensitive observers might have thought of as simply *empty,* such as Kuna.

In ancient Greece, everyone knew that Persephone, the daughter of Demeter, goddess of the earth and the harvest, was kidnapped by Hades, god of the Underworld (and coincidentally her uncle). Demeter blighted the earth till Hades let Persephone return, but she could come back for only half the year because she had eaten a few pomegranate seeds. So that's why we have seasons. I suppose the pomegranate seed is a metaphor for sex.

Mary's husband Arthur was no Hades, but he did work underground in mines a lot of the time. And Mary was a farmer's daughter, like Persephone (if one may label the goddess Demeter with that modest epithet). I'm sure Mary would have seen the possibilities of that particular extended metaphor. (Though perhaps her friend Helena would have found it more apt! Some evidence in the letters suggests that she found it hard to get over her resentment at Arthur for taking Mary away from the East, despite the fact that Mary went to her western exile willingly.) Human lives do follow these patterns, intended or not. People made myths to explain things that had already happened.

The Greeks knew a lot about nature, not just in the sense of utility. They even had a few mines, which Mary might have been interested in. (She became remarkably fluent in the language and lore of mines from reading to Arthur, who suffered from weak eyes.) But the Greeks had another relationship with nature. The ancients were the first eco-warriors. There are many myths about people being punished for cutting down sacred trees, rivers falling in love with human beings, human beings transformed into aspects of nature to save them from some disaster. (Only occasionally is being turned into something in nature a punishment, as in the case of Niobe, who was turned to stone for pride.) Nature was regarded as numinous and alive. The ancient world was a place in which the borders between worlds were thinner. Who is to say, at this remove, what was real, and what was not? One need only consider what the ancients might have thought about how we send our voices and pictures through the invisible air to realize that strangeness is relative.

I think the numinousness of the natural world, which was familiar to the ancients, is something that Mary felt instinctively and that she communicated obliquely in both her art and writing. I'm not suggesting Mary saw dryads and naiads in the woods, but that she had a sense of the spiritual potential of the natural world, and that the Quaker dictum to "rejoice in the splendor of God's continuing creation" had prepared her to see the world with open eyes. She wasn't quite a transcendentalist, being at heart a practical person, but she had certain things in common with them. Much of what she thought and felt is lost to us, "inside history" as she would have said. "Inside history": it's such a good term. So much of what she writes in her letters is "inside history," history that wouldn't have been evident in her day-to-day life: what is heard in the heart but never spoken. We all have our private histories, but a lot of it gets forgotten. Sometimes I wonder what I was doing during whole decades of my life. I've written a lot of it down, but Mary, in her effort to stay connected to her old world, wrote nearly *all* of it down.

Despite her appreciation for the new natural world she found herself in at New Almaden, Mary was nonetheless caught between worlds, as the exile so often is. One knows exactly what she felt in this circumstance:

> If I opened a trunk and took out a dress that had hung in the closets at home, waves of a faint, sickish emotion went over me. I didn't wish to go back, yet I could have cried with the pang of those odors released from its folds. Visions and voices from another world as different from this as my life was now from that girlhood to which I had died: "O perpetua fiori!"...These are not earthly odors. I thought then it was New Almaden and marriage and the dry season. (her ellipsis)[3]

This calling back of the past is something the exile knows well. Anyone who has left behind a history is distracted, if not troubled, when that history comes alive again, present once more. But Mary is right—one doesn't really want the past. I don't want to be eighteen again, living in my hometown. But when I go back to that place, walk up the stairs of my childhood home, hear the creak on every stair as I used to hear it, smell the scent of a 150-year-old wooden house that is imprinted on me like no other place on this earth, for a moment I can feel like I *am* eighteen—the age I was when I left home. The sense of being deeply embedded in my own history is almost too much to bear. It *is* too much to bear. I can't stay there for long, and yet it sometimes feels like the place I am meant to be. The light, the air, the trees, the views—Mount Tamalpais in one direction, Mount Diablo in the other—all haunt me. Late afternoon in Northern California—Northern California that Mary came to as a new wife, her first exile—is for me the exile's return. I'd almost rather be riding the Underground in London on a Monday morning in November—it doesn't demand so much of me. When I first read about Mary in Stegner's book, and thought of her long California days, her gold-bright California mornings, the weight of the heat of the endless afternoons, it all came back to me in a rush. What Mary knew as strange and new was *my* history, and until I read about Mary I had almost forgotten it.

I'm typing this on a plane, going back again, as Mary did, endlessly returning to one's place of origin, endlessly leaving it again. There's something mythic in the whole process, even though it's now accomplished in airplanes. It turns one's mind to look for parallels, to find congruences in what one does and what has always been done. It pulls us into history, all this traveling, our own and the world's.

Parallels

When she arrived in California, aged twenty-eight, just married, just having taken that leap into the unknown newness of life with a man she really didn't know well but trusted and loved, and a world about which she had few preconceptions, Mary was carrying the blocks for the illustrations to *The Scarlet Letter.*

The congruence of this commission is striking. There was Mary, lovely, charming, talented, intelligent, and open to her new life on the edge of a continent, making a home in the uncharted wilderness—maybe not quite uncharted, but new, at least compared with New York—during a time of expansion and possibility. And there was the beautiful Hester Prynne, protagonist of *The Scarlet Letter,* on the edge of another wilderness, one that would one day be full of possibility but which at her time was bound by the strictures of a repressive religious culture. Both women found society, such as it was, trying; both had a skill that set them apart; both took solace in wild places. Maybe that is where the congruences end, but as Adam Sonstegard notes in an insightful essay:

> This heroine, Hester Prynne, and this artist, Mary Hallock Foote, in fact, feature odd parallels, eerie correspondences. If the heroine moved early in her marriage to a location just emerging from the wilderness, the artist similarly moved in the early days of her marriage to California's remote mining camps. One found herself in that wilderness without her husband. The other had to have worried about feeling abandoned in a desolate, far western frontier.[4]

Mary clearly sympathized with Hester, despite her own inflexible moral code. In New Almaden she was a newly married woman, and she must have suffered for Hester, whatever nineteenth-century morality dictated. For Hester, like Mary, was in love, but Hester's love was hopeless. Yet the nineteenth century was not always as rigid as one might assume. Sonstegard states that Mary Hallock Foote "sketch[es] respectful screens around Hester, which Hawthorne's embedded Puritan audiences within the book pointedly do not respect."[5] And looking at Mary's illustrations in this edition of Hawthorne's novel, one sees, again and again, the depiction of a strong woman, full of integrity and fortitude, which mirrors the character we meet in the text.[6] But audiences have not always read *The Scarlet Letter* in the same way; Mary's interpretation feels decidedly modern. Sonstegard's meticulous reading adds enormously to the reader's understanding of both Hawthorne's novel and Mary's artistic integrity and skill.

The Madonna-like figure that is Hester Prynne in Mary Hallock Foote's illustrations echoes and enhances Hawthorne's text, and as Sonstegard notes, the respectful way in which Mary "screens" Hester from the harsh gaze of the unforgiving townspeople reveals her innate sympathies. Fully alive to Hester's predicament, Mary nonetheless understands social constraints, perhaps too well. Her depiction of the fatally

From Nathaniel Hawthorne, *The Scarlet Letter* (Boston: James R. Osgood and Co., 1878), 65.

weak and flawed Dimmesdale reveals her acceptance of the inevitability of the novel's conclusion, given the rigid cultural constraints of the time in which it is set.

Mary's vision of nature in this work is interesting too. One has to assume the backgrounds in the illustrations are based on the hills around New Almaden; it is striking how California in 1878 becomes New England in the seventeenth century. In her illustration of Hester and Dimmesdale in the forest, a California live oak stands behind the goddess-like figure of Hester—Artemis in the forest, next to the gnome-like Dimmesdale—here reminiscent of Chillingworth in his

From Nathaniel Hawthorne, *The Scarlet Letter* (Boston: James R. Osgood and Co., 1878), 257.

furtive posture, half-hidden behind the erect, noble figure of Hester. Mary doesn't have to tell us what she thinks of Dimmesdale; the picture says it all.

No, Mary wouldn't have cared much for the Arthur Dimmesdales of this world, crippled by weakness and fears, men with scruples but not strength. She was married to Arthur Foote, an upright, loving, and supportive husband. Perhaps not the best businessman, but honest, strong, brave, and true.

In a letter just before her first Christmas in the West, Mary wrote to Helena:

> December 22, 1876
> This is the strangest Christmas weather—wild and bright but soft as windy days in April. It is very late for the heavy rains to begin, and the greenness is fading for want of encouragement—The valley has been touched by frost and this blight added to the drought

> makes it look as if a flame had passed over it. We have only a few pale wreaths of fog these clear windy mornings—and they float low leaving the mountain line dark and sharply outlined against the most solemn radiant morning sky. The redwoods on a distant range of hills, stand out like spears or furled flags of a marching Army. There is always a distinctly masculine character about this Scenery—the Mountains are ominous and—even when all alight with color they seem to have a meaning with the shadow of some impending doom in it. The effect of *stillness* is wonderfully impressive. No matter how the wind may blow here—or the people clatter & cackle in their little houses—the light on the Mountains is always still as if they were part of another world—[7]

"Another world." How well she understood the reality of nature, that trees and mountains and running rivers do speak to us in a language that we may choose to hear, or not; speak to us and take us to that place where their language and presence is all there is, far away from the life of humanity, unless, as Mary has done, humanity goes to it. That is why I can never quite believe that Mary would have given up her western adventure for life back in the East. I think she derived comfort, at every moment of her western life, from the fact that she was living a life in nature. It was so much a part of her that she did not even need to write about it to Helena. It is there, always. One need only look at the many passages of luminous prose flowing out from the pages of her novels—novels mainly written to keep the pot boiling, often with market-driven forces controlling the plots and characterizations, but novels, and journalism, in which the voice of the true lover of the green world comes through nonetheless. Here are a few examples:

> Primeval life and love were all around them. Meadow larks flung their brief jets of song into the sunlight; the copses rustled with wings.... They had found their Garden.[8]

> But at night, all the teeming life of the plain rushed up into the sky and blazed there in a million friendly stars. After the languor of the sleepy afternoons, it was like a fresh awakening—the dawn of those white May nights.[9]

> The stillness of the desert closed about him with delicious healing. He was a world-weary child returned to the womb of Nature.[10]

> And then the wind would blow, and no heart not strong in happiness could bear that senseless riot and rapture, prolonged throughout the night, under wild reaches of midnight sky, under the white stride of the Milky Way; with soundings of the river's stops; with whisperings amidst the poplars' dusky files—cowled shapes against the dark, closing and parting, with rifts of stars in between.[11]

> But you'd not think small things of our Sand Springs Fall by night, that glimmers on the dark cliff opposite—cliff, and mist-like cataract, and the low moon throwing the shadow of the bluff across it, all repeated in the stiller, darker picture of the lagoon. I shall not inflict much of this sort of thing upon you; but the senseless beauty of it all gives one a heartache.[12]

> Desert did not seem the word for this country, nor was it deserted—it was just coming into being after some long creative pause.[13]

There is both familiarity and awe in these descriptions: intimacy and profound respect; and some expressions stand out: "riot and rapture," "senseless beauty." This sense of being enraptured by nature, *taken over* by it, is not particular to Mary among writers of the western landscape; one hears similar passion in John Muir's writings, albeit in a somewhat more reverential, slightly less intimate voice. But there is a sense in both writers of transcendental astonishment.

Many times in her letters we hear exclamations of what Mary feels is her inadequacy of expression in these new circumstances, particularly in reference to the landscape. Early on in her western sojourn, she writes of the rural setting of New Almaden:

> July 18, 1876
> We are as retired as if there were no mine within a hundred miles—all we can see of the outside world is the bit of winding road which disappears round a curve of the hill beneath an arching young live oak tree and the roofs & gables of two or three miners' cottages half hidden by trees. We are as much alone as if we were in

> a light-house—and it makes me think of that when we look out in front down the cliff where the valley lies below as level as the sea—and the mountains rising all around, some in shadow some in light. In the early morning the valley is like a great lake, filled with fog which rises in waves—rolling up—sometimes blown off in light drifts—I can give you no idea of the view.[14]

But thank you Mary, you have given us a splendid idea of the view, or as close to an idea as one can have at a distance of 140 years, and, as I read it in London, five thousand miles removed.

Mary Hallock Foote frequently personifies aspects of the natural world in her writing—and not just in the usual romantic or quasi-mythological ways that the nineteenth century was comfortable with. She takes the landscape in and understands it in a way that seems to belong to no particular age: her sensibility is not strictly romantic. As I have previously noted, there are elements of transcendentalist thought in hers, but Mary does not take the purely cerebral, rather masculine approach of most of those thinkers. Her understanding seems both personal and female, an understanding that comes from deep in the self, the soul.

To suggest that the female understanding of the world is different from the male's is not without its dangers, but consider Annette Kolodny's thoughts on this in *The Land Before Her*:

> Like their husbands and fathers, women too shared in the economic motives behind emigration; and like the men, women also dreamed of transforming the wilderness. But the emphases were different.
>
> After initial reluctance at finding themselves on the wooded frontiers . . . women quite literally set about planting gardens in these wilderness places. . . . Avoiding for a time male assertions of a rediscovered Eden, women claimed the frontiers as a potential sanctuary for an idealized domesticity. Massive exploitation and alteration of the continent do not seem to have been part of women's fantasies. They dreamed, more modestly, of locating a home and a familial community within a cultivated garden.[15]

Invested as she was in Arthur's plans, and freed by her profession from the more arduous aspects of pioneer life, this was not entirely Mary's view. In fact, she preferred to be away from the settlements and positively reveled in the wild landscapes, despite paradoxically longing for the settled domestic sphere she had left behind. But what Mary loved was not domesticity as such but the beautiful textures of a lived-in world, the detail of it, the warp and weft, as Kolodny states. Her early sketches illustrating farm life in her home of Milton, New York, show this.

In one Vermeer-like scene, titled *Gathering Butter,* which appeared in "Picturesque Aspects of Farm Life in New York," the sense of the beauty and dignity of Mary's old life is evident.[16] The light shines into the pantry through leaded glass windows; there is a trellis outside, and a plant, perhaps a climbing rose, is framed in the deep-set alcove. The woman gathering the butter from the barrel churn does not look like a miserable, overworked domestic skivvy; rather, her countenance exudes patience and serenity. She is nearly done, in any case; the butter bowl is overflowing. This peaceful stillness is also characteristic of Mary's depictions of the natural world. Even in those that show a less than serene natural world, the human figures are almost always in repose, watchful, calm.

Yet western domestic spheres were raw compared to those Mary had left in the East. And while nature was grand, it was not a lived-in world to her. She had to become reconciled with the natural world on a different footing. But Mary's attachment to her native place and family occupation never wavered. *The Royal Americans,* a historical novel published in 1910, the first significant work she did after the death of her beloved daughter Agnes, is set in Revolutionary-era New York, in an area she knew well. Describing the character of Charlotte, an orphan who has been raised by Native Americans, Mary writes:

> She walked or ran as a bird from the snare. Her youth had come back, and peace like a foretaste of heaven was in the present of this new, free, innocent home....
>
> She was in the forest alone once more, in the silence no wood lover can forget, with that immeasurable joy, awake and pulsating, that comes with a night of perfect spring.[17]

Several things are evident in this excerpt. Passion for nature and deep understanding of its healing power are clear. Joy is there; one cannot describe an emotion one hasn't felt. This is Mary's voice, returning after the dark years of mourning her daughter, and returning, significantly, in description of the natural world. Like a wood nymph, or dryad, with a sensibility like that of an ancient Greek, Charlotte finds peace in nature; so too, in some sense, does her creator. Later in the same work Mary talks about the cultivation of the landscape, in language that only one who had known the land on intimate terms could use:

> Suppose that *we* had cut this field out of the immensity of the forest, and planted this wonderful beauty for a sign of the work of the husbandman; his care for his family and the poor, and his forethought for the winter. Farming is creation! Are you not proud to be a farmer, Francis?[18]

I think of Mary writing these words in 1910, for the first of two historical novels, remembering her young life as the daughter of a farmer. Her life had taken her far from those roots, though she still lived—always lived, in fact, except for a spell in New York during art school—in close proximity to nature. It is suggestive of the deep bond she kept with her native place, and the natural world overall, that when she returned to writing after the greatest tragedy of her life, it was to these scenes that she returned. Nature heals. It also nurtures. As a child, Mary had been nurtured in the arms of a domesticated natural world. In her youthful work, one sees nature modified by humanity. Her more mature drawings show humans *in* nature, never *in control* of it. She embraced a more free and wild natural world as an adult woman. Some of her early illustrations reveal this early appreciation and understanding.[19]

Mary and Arthur spent only a little over a year at New Almaden, but it made a deep impression on her. It was her first western sojourn and her first experience of being away from her eastern milieu and in a new domestic framing of life. This first spell in California also gave an idea of the kind of things Arthur had to put up with—corrupt labor practices, bullying bosses, and extremely hard work. They lasted only a little over a year there, not because Arthur found it too hard, but because he had too much integrity and would not collude with his autocratic superior on several matters, including ill treatment of the miners.

Although she loved a lot of things about her new life, there were certainly moments when Mary was overwhelmed with nostalgia and homesickness for her old world. She described one such moment in a letter to Helena:

> March 10, 1877
> I did not know how much I had missed the birds until one evening Arthur returned from a ride to San Jose—It was in Feb. just after a long mild rain. He said he wished so much that I could have been with him riding through the valley at sunset—"The meadow-larks were singing." That was all he said, but Hy it brought back a pang of home sickness—Just for a minute, I felt as if I "couldn't stay." What is it like, I wonder not to care for one place more than another. There are so many people here who do not understand what I mean, when I talk of home and the East.[20]

This sort of wave that washes over one at times is something most exiles know. It can be evoked by anything: the scent of flowering jasmine could almost reduce me to tears when I was first married and knew I had finally cast my lot with the English; there was a street in my hometown filled with jasmine plants. I used to walk home from school that way just to smell them.

Sometimes music will do it. Driving down a country lane in Hampshire (old, not New), a song I knew in my university days came on the radio. At the next turn, I found myself driving on the wrong side of the road—the right, as if I was in California.

Visitors can prompt it too. An old friend arrives. After the late-night conversations, the visits to the local sights, the surprise that you both now have gray hair, you wonder, how did that happen? How did those years fall away so quickly? But then you remember. You went away. The sense that one has left something undone in the past is hard to escape.

But going home is not easy either. When I return to California, my first sense is always how things have changed. One instantly notices differences. In my hometown, a building has been changed, another built, another torn down; the roads have been narrowed/widened/made one way. A favorite restaurant has changed its interior, or exterior, or disappeared entirely. Farther afield, yet another new shopping mall has blighted the once lovely, pale brown hills that roll down toward the Bay, home in the past to ranches and the typical brown-and-white Hereford cattle that are a common sight in Northern California. I remember seeing for the first time the glossy-coated black-and-white cows that populate the ever-green pastures of southern England. They looked like pictures in a child's storybook. At twenty-one, I think I still thought all cows had the rough, shaggy coats of those at home and that all hills were parched until December.

But it's not just things that have changed; people have too; and most significantly I have changed. I am no longer the twenty-one-year-old who packed her bags and left for England, for Spain, for marriage, for children, for sickness and health, and all the rest of it. For life. I wish I could identify the feeling I get when I go back. Is it sadness? Is it nostalgia? Is it a kind of happiness? Certainly, I'm always glad to be back. And I'm usually a little bit reluctant to return to England because going back is the end of vacation. I'm going back to the job, the house, the thousand and one things one has to do to live one's life. But in a day or two I'll be having coffee with a friend in the café in the park; walking home, over the top of the hill, looking at the rooftops and the Thames in the glittering afternoon light, and thinking, "This is fine. This is more than fine, this is wonderful." And then I might look at the photographs of the trip just gone and think about that late afternoon California light, and it begins again. Circles. So, I return to Edward Said's description of exile: "It is the unhealable rift forced between a human being and a native place, between the self and its true home: its essential sadness can never be surmounted."[21] Although the sadness fades somewhat, it's always an undercurrent, something Mary, and I, would live with for many years.

CHAPTER THREE

Leadville

IN THEIR NEXT long western sojourn, Mary and Arthur went to Leadville, Colorado. Before that, there had been six months in Santa Cruz and thirteen months for Mary back in Milton while Arthur scouted out work, first in Deadwood, then Leadville. When they finally reunited, Mary left their son with her family for six months. Although she had hated being separated from Arthur, the separation from her child must have been traumatic. It's hard to imagine the choices Mary had to make. So it's good to know that she loved Leadville. And after six months she and Arthur returned to Milton and brought their little boy back with them.

Mary's first view of Colorado was dramatic. She wrote to Helena:

> May 12, 1879
> The mountain road, the pines were grand—but the South Park! That was my great surprise! I had expected a flat barren plain—It is a glorious sweep of rolling hills—with clumps of trees where they most fitly mark the distance of the great mountain chain which encircles the high rolling plain. It seemed a playground for the Centaurs—so vast, so brilliant, so free and utterly unspoilable. There were the dark pine covered mountains and beyond the Snowy range—awful, beautiful, unreal!—When Arthur told me that before next night we would have crossed both the dark mountains and the dazzling formidable white one I could not believe it.[1]

The imagery must have appealed to her—the dark and white mountains opposed to one another, like great mythic presences. And entering into that world, despite her misgivings, would have roused the soul of adventure in her. At those times, Mary must have entered into her new environment with some contradictory feelings, fear not least, but also with a kind of thrill at the sheer *otherness* of the place she had come to. She was alive to every place she went, and expressed the complexity of her thoughts not only in her letters to Helena but also later in her novels. In *John Bodewin's Testimony,* a tale of Colorado, she gives these sentiments to one of her less resilient female characters:

> The mountains themselves had, to her morbid fancy, an oppressive individuality. They intruded upon her, in the midst of her small, subtle joys and pains of today, with their heart-breaking stolidity and their immense past. They took meaning out of her efforts, and made them seem of no avail.[2]

I don't think this was Mary's experience in Colorado. Not that she was always on a Rocky Mountain high during her Leadville time; she must have had low points, particularly when she was missing her little son. But there was a grandeur, and romance too, in western places, which Mary felt almost immediately in her western experience. It was a feeling and an understanding inspired in part by the rhetoric of western expansion, but more significantly by the land itself. In *John Bodewin's Testimony,* again, she writes:

> Its hopes [the mountain settlement] and its capital were largely bound up in the fate of adventurers into that unpeopled land which has no history except the records written in fire, in ice, in water, on its rocks and river-beds; the voyagers across that inland sea where the smoke of lonely camp-fires goes up from wagon-roads that were once hunter's trails, and trails that were once the tracks of buffalo.[3]

In the pronounced absence of acknowledgment of any Native American presence in the land, Mary reveals her own and her culture's limitations. What she does write of is that western places were at least initially dependent for their existence on individual endeavor, and that endeavor was linked to an intimate relationship with the land. Records "written in fire, in ice, in water, on . . . rocks and river-beds" are records of human endurance and suffering, and yes, of triumph too. But there is not only grandeur; there is also intimacy:

> They were hovering about in that fascinating borderland between firelight and moonlight. The moon had risen high enough to fill the thin woods with its light; but it was a pale, suffused radiance

by contrast with the red fire-glow. The wind in the tree-tops over their heads, like a circle of unseen whisperers, closed around the lightly joined thread of their talk.

"Do people ever get used to this?" Josephine asked.[4]

In this I think we hear Mary's true feelings, feelings that may have begun tentatively but when fully formed never lost their intensity in her deep and abiding love for the natural world of the West. There is an understanding of nature and a deep personal connection and awareness of *presence*—"unseen whisperers." She was utterly alive to her surroundings and open to what the land would say to her at all times, despite her misgivings about being so far from her home.

I'd like to talk to Mary, to sit next to her as she sketches a Rocky Mountain vista and see what's in her mind. How can I do that? Imagine being there...

I'm standing on one side of an opaque barrier called history. I can see a figure on the other side, looking at the undrawn landscapes surrounding her. How do I get through? And yet, now I am through. I am there, walking over to where Mary sits sketching. I sit down. She doesn't look at me, absorbed in what she's doing or simply not interested in an interloper 140 years out of time.

"Thee asks too many questions."

I'm startled. I didn't expect her to speak to me first. I didn't think I had spoken, but did I? I wouldn't have thought I merited the familiar "Thee," either.

But no, there's someone else Mary is talking to, half lying on the hillside, holding a book, his back to her. He's looking at the book but looking at the view too. A young man, one of her minders I suppose. Arthur never let her wander around alone where she might get bothered by any of the rough Leadville types. Is this Pricey—the young Englishman who followed Mary around like a lost puppy when she lived in Leadville? Perhaps. Too innocuous to be a serious threat to anyone who was intent on trouble, but a presence nonetheless. She liked him. He was well educated; he had been to Oxford and could talk about books, quote poetry. She continues talking, almost to herself. "But since thee asks, I'll tell thee. It was hard, yes, terribly hard leaving New York, leaving the baby at home with the family. But I couldn't leave Arthur here alone any longer. And there was this to come to." She gestures with a sweep of her hand at the view. Nearly two miles high, there are some spectacular views around Leadville.

I think perhaps she's drawing a picture that she later used in her Colorado novel, *The Led-Horse Claim*. It's a scene of the Rockies, towering over what looks like a line of toy wagons, descending into the shadow of the mountains. It's a lot like one she drew for the cover of the January 1879 issue of *Scribner's*. That must be the Rockies too, the Rockies with Vikings.

It would be nice to know the stories of the two pictures. She certainly knew something about these landscapes—we can see it in the way she captures that ominous quality of the descent taking place in the second picture, in which we see only the backs of the Vikings, as we see only the backs of the wagons in the picture for *The Led-Horse Claim*.[5] In both pictures there is a descent, to be followed by a precipitous rise. It looks like the Vikings are going toward a sunrise, while the wagons are heading for evening. In both pictures the landscapes have a kind of foreknowledge of what is to come.

I'd like to ask her. She's sitting, looking at that view. She's got a serious look on her face. Pricey is back at his book. It's Emerson. She looks intently; she's almost transfigured for a moment by the depths of her concentration and observation. She wrote something in her reminiscences that captures this mood:

> The mountains of the Great Divide are not, as everyone knows, born treeless though we always think of them as far above timberline with the eternal snow on their heads. They wade up through ancient forests and plunge into cañons tangled up with watercourses and pause in little gem-like valleys and march attended by loud winds across high plateaus, but all such incidents of the lower world they leave behind them when they begin to strip for the skies: like the Holy Ones of old, they go up alone and barren of all circumstance, to meet their transfiguration.[6]

There is in this passage, once again, the evocative idea of transfiguration. And the personification of nature, which is so often a feature of her writing, is there too in a very personal way, as though she'd waded and plunged, paused, as one with the mountains, and gone heavenward.

Cover picture, *Scribner's*, January 1879.

I think this quality is why her nature pictures, like her nature writing, are so effective—it's as if she is living the life of the trees or the mountains or the rivers she writes about: her connection with the natural world is personal.

I want to say, "Mary, what does it mean to you?" but I don't have to. Pricey stammers, "Mrs. Foote"—they were a formal lot back then—"Mrs., Mrs. Foote..."

"Yes, Pricey?"

"Emerson talks about natural facts being symbols of spiritual facts."

"Yes, in *Nature*."

"Then what do we really make of the fact that while nature can be beautiful, it can also be terrible?" he asks, warming to his subject.

"He says that nature is the symbol of spirit," she says, looking at the range across the valley where thunderheads have begun to appear.

"Yes," Pricey replies.

"Well, if we accept that, then we have to accept that the spirit can be terrible too. I don't mean bad, or wicked, I mean terrible, awful, frightening."

"Sublime?"

"Yes, as Mr. Burke defines it," she replied.

"But we, people, are rarely sublime, except in our aspirations." Pricey doesn't stammer now; he never did when he was talking about philosophy.

"No, not often, but even having our aspirations may be enough..."

The thunderheads gathering across the valley crack resoundingly.

"We better get back, Pricey," she says, gathering her skirts around her as she stands.

Pricey jumps up and begins to gather Mary's things—sketching stool, basket. They hurry away down the path as the first bolt of lightning strikes.

The storm has passed, and here comes Arthur, walking home from the mine office where he spends his days when he's not surveying underground. He was talking to another man just now, someone from the mines. That man has turned back, and Arthur continues up the path to home. He's a big, good-looking man. He's got a pipe in his mouth, but he's not smoking it. He strides up the seventy-degree angle of the hillside as if he were walking down a garden path. Here he comes. He stops. I'd like to ask him how it felt being out here alone, waiting for Mary, wondering if she'd ever come. He stops and lights his pipe. He turns and looks down the valley from which he's just ascended like a spirit rising. He smiles. He laughs. He must have good news. And he's a young man, full of energy and joy, going home to a wife he adores. He continues on his way back to their cabin.

Back at the cabin Mary is telling Pricey something. He hurries off to do her bidding. She smiles. It's early in their stay here, before they've brought little Arthur back from New York, where he is being looked after by Mary's sister, Bessie. Arthur comes in. Lots of hugging and kissing. Mary laughs and pushes him away. She's a little older than him, and it shows. He's still a bit boyish. People are coming in the evening he tells her; mock alarm as she looks around the one-room cabin that will have the same function as one of her friend Helena's elegant New York salons. No matter.

The evening arrives. The cabin is full of light and talk, glasses of wine and smoke of cigars. Arthur doesn't say a lot. Mary is the only woman. She is often the center of attention, and she talks "a blue streak" much to the pleasure of the men, all of whom seem to adore her too. The evening is lively and merry. Some drink too much, but no one gets sloppy. Everyone drifts away about eleven. Mary and Arthur sit and look at each other, smiling. The door to the cabin is open, and the smell of cigar and pipe smoke is already nearly gone, but a pleasant undertone lingers on the crisp night air.

There were many evenings like this, as we know from Mary's memoirs and letters. It is staggering to think how free they must have felt, how grand the West must have seemed, that it could give them both kinds of life: the new world of the West, and the old world—at a remove, yes, but still there in their hearts.

So far, so good. Mary and Arthur in Leadville—with one child. Mary still working: writing, drawing, and painting. Nothing bad had happened yet. They were soon to go to Mexico on what Mary considered their one big romantic adventure; their whole life seems like one big romantic adventure to me! Arthur was not a resounding financial success, but he'd done well in his field and was respected. Troubles hadn't come to call—not yet. Stay there! I want to say. Stay in that high, clear air. Take the job you've been offered with the U.S. Geological Survey, Arthur; nothing better is going to come along for a while. Who knows where you'll end up living. But Arthur can't hear me, and Mary will go along with his plans; she was nothing if not an extraordinarily supportive wife—as he was an extraordinarily supportive husband. They were well matched.

The spell in Colorado resonates through Mary's life. It was their West at its best: spectacular scenery, congenial friends, youth, love, hope. Nostalgia for that bit of their western dream resonates throughout Mary's life. She wrote three novels about it, *The Led-Horse Claim, John Bodewin's Testimony, The Last Assembly Ball,* and several stories. The sublimity of the landscape was two-sided, however. As in New Almaden, when she wrote of the mountains, "waiting there, patient, unpitying, eternal," so too does the fabulous mountain scenery around Leadville draw from her an ambivalence revealing an awareness of the unknowableness, the inexplicable profundity, the sense of implacable *presence* called forth by nature.

When she was back in Milton, between Leadville and Mexico, she wrote the following to Helena. Disingenuously referring to her feelings as "paltry," she attempts to convey the magnitude of her emotions in the presence of a natural world that seems to have almost an *awareness,* expressed in its "Sphynx-like calm":

> April 1882
> You will think me too silly, if I confess how much I feel it—for it is such a paltry thing! But the merest hint of those tremendous impressions, which would have roused my genius once for all, if I had any, affects me with that same closing of the heart, as in the presence of some impending Fate.
>
> The snow peaks, with the shadow of the opposite range climbing their sides at sunset, leaving their gleaming sierras in sharp light against the sky. The lonely trail winding wearily—lost, reappearing—disappearing at last—enfolded in the long spurs of the range descending into the valley—vanishing at the entrance to the pass. There is awful temerity in the advance of a handful of men with their flimsy accompaniments into these solitudes—"That desolate land and lone." It has no human history. There is something appalling to me in the blank silence of those immeasurable unrecorded ages that there lie exposed—no not unrecorded—but I cannot read their dumb tablets of rock—I only feel the Sphynx-like calm which seems to ask you how you expect to live there—If you cannot answer the problem, retreat or death are the alternatives and it makes no difference to anything earthly, there, which you choose.[7]

How one wishes she would not minimize the depth of her understanding in making her perceptions clear to Helena, who for all her sophistication would never have got beyond the "picturesque" in her understanding of a West that Mary read so deeply! The thing I love about Mary's observations is the fact that she acknowledges when she is dealing with the inexplicable, when she has got to Butala's "place where words stop." I believe this place is actually *more* than the "sublime," but it is the place where words stop, so "sublime" will have to do.

I use the term *sublime* in a modified Burkean sense. The sublime, according to Burke, partakes of the terrifying, the vast, the magnificent, the powerful, the loud, the painful, and so on: "It is productive of the strongest emotion which the mind is capable of feeling."[8] This description fits the monumental, inspiring, strange, and sometimes bizarre western landscapes so frequently approached by painters such as Bierstadt, Moran, and Church. But I believe that Mary's sensibility goes further. In *West of Everything,* Jane Tompkins writes of an environment that is "inimical to human beings." She continues:

> But the negations of the physical setting...are also its siren song. Be brave, be strong enough to endure this and you will become like this—hard, austere, sublime. This code of asceticism founds our experience of Western stories.[9]

Sublimity in this sense is clearly *not* the same as beauty, attractiveness, or the picturesque; and while the sublime in nature may be beautiful, it is not necessarily so. The sublime in landscapes, particularly western American landscapes, has to do with their effect on the viewer, which I suggest is something even beyond the "delightful horror" posited by nineteenth-century landscape painters in their interpretations of the sublime in landscape. The imaginative effect of landscape, the capacity to lift the mind to a level of contemplation that brings it closer to an understanding of the divine, transforms the viewer. Their capacity to transform character gives certain landscapes a sentience, which I believe Mary knew and understood, and which some of her best writing approaches.

Mary did not often try to draw sublime landscapes, not really. Her drawings tend to be of the less spiritually demanding landscapes—not that they were not challenging in their own ways. Landscapes such as those depicted in *Looking for Camp* or *The Coming of Winter,* both drawn for the series Pictures of the Far West, which appeared in *Century* during 1888-89, are *knowable* landscapes, unlike the *sublime* landscapes she refers to in her letter and in some other writings.

In these, as in many of her western landscapes, Mary gives us a feminized landscape. That is not simply to say she places women in the landscape—often she does not—but rather that she creates landscapes in which the feminine is as real as the masculine, and the feminine gaze is that which interprets the landscape, unlike so often in western art when the male gaze is the only interpretation available. Consider her description of *Looking for Camp,* which appeared in the November 1889 issue of *Century* as part of the Pictures of the Far West series:

Looking for Camp, in Pictures of the Far West series, *Century,* November 1889.

The Coming of Winter, in Pictures of the Far West series, *Century,* December 1888.

> Of all the monotonous phases of the western landscape these high, solitary pastures are the most poetic. Nothing human is suggested by the plains except processions of tired people passing over, tribal movements, war parties, discoverers, and fortune-seekers. But the sentiment of the hills is restful. Their stillness is not lifeless; it is as if these warm-bosomed slopes were listening, like a mother to her child's breathing, for sounds from all the shy, wild communities which they feed and shelter—the slow tread of grazing herds, the call of a bird, the rustle of the stiff grass on the hill slopes, the lapsing trickle of water in gulches hidden by willows, and traced by their winding green from far across the dry slopes.[10]

The drawing that accompanied this piece centers our vision not so much on the man in the landscape but on the grasses that obscure his feet and the horse's hooves; the land bears them on sufferance; the moon watches, noncommittally. Only the man goes forward; both the horse and the dog are reluctant. The dog stands, the horse has to be pulled, the man walks forward in a posture suggestive of uncertainty. This looks like a photograph, or posed. I know Mary did draw from photos at times. She might have asked one of Arthur's assistants to pose for her. I wonder what her message to the man in the picture was?

"Mr. Wiley, try to look as if you are a little bit uneasy," she might have said. "It's getting late, and you don't know where you are going to sleep. You can see the river down below, so you are not too worried, but the horse has taken a stone in its hoof and is limping."

He's got his gun out, so he can shoot something—jackrabbit?—if he sees it. It doesn't look as if he's carrying anything to eat on his saddle. There's just a bedroll. He's a bit uncertain, but not truly worried. The days of the Indian wars are in the past, and as Mary says, the landscape is restful, ready to feed and shelter another wanderer. This gives us an entirely new vision of the West, one accessible to her female readers, which was not the case before Mrs. Foote came on the scene. In *The Coming of Winter,* Mary nails her colors to the mast even more definitively. In both the descriptive text that accompanies the drawing and in the drawing itself, the man is feckless. The cabin is inadequate to face the winter, and yet the man is not repairing it. Rather, he is dressed for hunting, as his despondent wife looks on, carrying a baby.

The text that accompanies this picture is even more damning, speaking of the settler's "brilliant" eye as he listens to the tales of westering pioneers even more feckless than he. Mary describes the wife's feelings: "She is not so sure of the marksman's aim as she would have been a year before she married him."[11] This understated remark says all. Mary is not entirely unsympathetic to the settler, though she acknowledges his weakness:

> He is losing time; he yearns for the spring and the dawn of new chances. But he is a restless, not a resolved man, and with spring comes back the birds of promise, the valley rings with their music, the seeds are up in the garden, and the baby is learning to walk.[12]

This final line sums up Mary's point of view perfectly. One can imagine her saying not quite gently to the settler in her picture, "You're thinking of moving on? After your wife has gone through the winter, with a new baby in the house? Now you can fix the floor and the windows. The baby needs a safe place to play. The garden is coming up. What are you thinking of?" And one can imagine the settler sheepishly hanging his head at the justice of Mary's words.

Leadville didn't last. It couldn't. Like so many western adventures, the beauty of it was in the transitory nature of the enterprise. But Arthur's mine work, ending with a proper western gunfight (though Arthur was not himself involved), made Leadville one of the more colorful stories the Footes had to tell. Mary's wry comment in her memoirs covers what must have been disappointment, though hardly heartbreak: "And now we were back to our bold beginnings once more and the tale of our last campaign sounded like a wild and silly dream told to those quiet faces at home."[13]

CHAPTER FOUR

Mexico

MEXICO! What was that like for the Quaker woman who'd never been anywhere, as she said herself? She writes that she "got together her sketching tools, packed a steamer trunk... and was off for the 'gulfs enchanted where the siren sings.'"[1] That it had a huge significance in Mary's life is evident in her recollection: "There it glows, a spot of intenser color in memory's painted windows that look toward sunset, riveting the eye amidst lower tones of burnt-out forests and dry deserts and old, fenced-in farms."[2] This metaphor deserves a word at least, casually placed as it is in Mary's memoirs between practical matters of who would look after the baby and how Arthur persuaded his employers to agree to her coming along on a working trip. This intensely visual image is arresting, so perfectly does it capture the mental synesthesia of remembrance. One can imagine the vividness and color of that remembrance for Mary, who spent her life, as she says, amid burnt-out forests, deserts, and old farms. Well, not quite. There was New York City, the Rocky Mountains, the beautiful high country of Boise Canyon, California, in the glory days... However, the metaphor is a useful one to point out the overall contrast between Mary's hardworking life, generally, and her moment in Mexico. If Mary could have seen Venice! Or Rome! Even London. What then? But she appreciated what she had; and who knows, perhaps her deep understanding of the natural world around her would not have been so acute had she filled her mind with ruins and wonders. Her way of seeing, like Jane Austen's, depended on the careful study of the seemingly ordinary. But there was nothing ordinary about her trip to Mexico.

Mary wrote up her Mexican journey for Richard Gilder, who published three articles by her between November 1881 and March 1882. I can find no letters relating to this trip, so whether the post was so uncertain that Mary did not write, or the letters she did write went to the *Century* and were lost, we do not know. My hunch is that she wrote as she traveled but did not indulge in her usual many-leaved letters to Helena, knowing Helena would read the polished versions of her travels when Richard published them. And, having her adventure, Mary did not need to write as she usually did. (There are fewer letters from Leadville as well. This suggests, more than anything, that letter writing was a form of coping.) Her time was full; she was in the midst of new sights and sounds and experiences as far from her previous life as can be imagined. And she drew! The three published accounts contain twenty-three drawings, and there were undoubtedly more. She was thrilled and enchanted:

> The season was late January, but triumphant spring in the old city of Cortez—clear, intense sunlight, young leaves spreading, a commotion of birds in the city gardens, and a damp, earthy smell mingled with the perfume of violets. There was a thrill in the air which "stirs the blood with the instinct of travel," and gives one a longing to "tarnish the blue of distant mountains with one's feet."[3]

For one who had not traveled abroad, Mary certainly had the language for it. Her artist's powers of observation are evident from the outset. Listen to her description of a Mexican street:

> The houses in this part of the street have an individuality and a strong facial expression which impresses an American vividly in contrast to the monotonous, wide-eyed stare of a respectable New York street; each house is worthy of a description which would apply to no other.... The houses repose behind their crumbling garden-walls, looking out upon the shifting world of the street with a dull, slumberous dignity which ignores the pathetic look of social decadence and general decadence creeping over them.[4]

Mary imbues the street with life and personality, seeing what another might pass by unaware. She gives it qualities that contrast with those her audience might be familiar with, thus heightening the sense of the exotic.

Her trip to Mexico was Mary's Odyssey. She even remarks, "The Indian laborers whom we met all said, '*Buenos dias,*' and lifted their great hats and their great eyes to us, with the stare of one of Circe's beasts. Somewhere, you feel, in that dull body a man is imprisoned."[5] (One might expect such a thought to lead her to consider why the laborers, virtual slaves, were as they were. But she was of her age. Her social conscience extended as far as slavery, but wage slavery would have to wait for later voices to condemn it.) Indeed, there is also something Greek in her description of the ladies of Morelia at their afternoon "paseo":

> Powder is used without reserve or the slightest consideration for that subtle harmony which nature preserves between hair, eyes, and complexion. The effect is that of being surrounded by feminine masks, with beautiful human eyes looking out from them with an intensity of expression very startling in its contrast to the blank, soulless surface of faintly rouged white which the face presents.[6]

It seems that Mary was inclined to view Mexico in mythic terms—not surprisingly. It was as exotic a place as she had ever been. Those powdered faces sound like the tragic masks of Greek drama. I wonder if Mary knew of that tradition, from *Century* or *Scribner's*?

It was here in Mexico that Mary expresses some of the only opinions we ever hear her make about the rights of women:

> I wearied myself with speculations about the faces we had seen on the *paséo*—women's faces that permitted you one moment to look into a heart as deeply dyed as the *flor de noche buena,* and then shut you out with a sweep of the long lashes, and left you gazing at a dull, pretty, expressionless, powdered face.... What measure of content dwells with those cloistered lives, submitting and helping suicidally to preserve the conventions of a society which holds towards all women a consistent attitude of suspicion[?]... Such gayety as an American girl of the most reserved type enjoys, a Mexican girl could not conceive of. Nor could an American girl understand how it is possible to be as bright and sweet-tempered and patient as many—almost all—young Mexican girls are upon such frugal spiritual and mental cheer.[7]

I'm glad that Mary noticed this and sympathized. Sometimes it seems that social issues pass her by. (But then, as far as I am aware, neither did Jane Austen comment on the conditions of the poor, or the continued tacit acceptance of slavery in Britain even after its abolition.)

What this implies is that as a writer she lived within her own milieu, a sheltered one, despite her western travels. And Mary was of a conservative bent, though not so much as the Gilders, by whom she was influenced. (I think of her treatment of the "Coxeyites" in her short story "The Trumpeter," who staged a kind of latter-day Peasants' Revolt, for which she had no sympathy; or her treatment of strikers in her novel *Coeur D'Alene.*[8] She had no truck with mob violence, which the mining disputes in Idaho looked like to her. At this distance, it would be very difficult to judge Mary's politics. She was not thoughtless or unfeeling in any way, simply very much of her time and class.) Additionally, she sees the Mexicans in historical terms:

> Even Humbolt [*sic*]...speaks of this national sadness. Nor can it be wondered at in a people who had the awful drama of human sacrifices for their amusement during one long, dark epoch.... The muscles which encircle the mouth (parenthesis-like), springing from the root of the nostril, have in the Indian face, that thickened rigid look which we see in the head of a Medusa, or the tragic mask.[9]

With the reference to Medusa and the tragic mask, she again returns to the mythic. Indeed, the entire journey from Morelia to Mexico City becomes Odyssean; the travelers stop for hospitality at great houses along the way, as Odysseus would have asked for xenia on his journeys.[10]

The journey was sheer romance for Mary. On the opening page of "A Diligence Journey in Mexico," the first of her three long pieces for *Century,* she writes:

> Beyond the mountain wall which encompasses the valley of Mexico there lay an interior full of indefinite promise; strange figures walked the streets of the capitol, or camped in its market-places, who had come over the mountains on their sandal-shod feet from a country of which travelers said, "There is nothing stranger out of Egypt."[11]

Reading this, we know we are in a land of magic and mystery. The diligence driver looks like a satyr; the ancient paving stones hint at a far distant past; everything is suffused with the mystery of a little understood antiquity.

And still, everything is seen with the eye of the artist. Departing on the early morning stage for Maravitio, farther in the interior, Mary writes:

> The man who sits beside the driver carried a torch, made of agave rope, covered in pitch; by its yellow glare, the unfamiliar landscape was revealed in sudden flashes framed in darkness. We had left the tumult of the pavements and gained the silent country road.[12]

We are there, with her. We see the strange, cinematic landscape appear and vanish in this wonderful visual image. The contrast of the city pavements with the quiet country road is a graceful touch. Not only do we see what Mary saw, we hear the silence; we sense the darkness, illuminated briefly by the "yellow glare" of the torch. Mary, who has never left America, is in the heart of a world as exotic as anything her much-traveled New York friends ever saw.

Mary's way of seeing is a combination of the artist's and the writer's. Again, like Jane Austen, she had an eye for the small, yet revealing detail in behavior and in people. But more than Austen, because she was an artist, trained in observation, she *saw* every bit of the actual world around her, and is able to give it to us in her drawings as well as in her prose. The illustration *A Country Store,* which appeared in the first of Mary's three pieces, is a case in point. The stone wheels of the battered bullock cart, the burdened woman carrying her water jar, saddleless ponies and their keeper in his short tunic, the mangy dog, the general air of age and neglect combined with an antique elegance make this scene fascinating and memorable. We could be anywhere in the undeveloped world, in any time; but certainly, again the ancient world comes to mind. As I have said, there are many comparisons to the ancient Greeks in these three pieces. I think that ancient world was perhaps the only comparison she could draw on; and it's an apt one. The ancient world was a brutal, beautiful, implacable place. So was Mexico at the time Mary was there, and so are many places still. In seeing it for the first time, Mary gives it a freshness and immediacy. She shows us things she might have not seen had she been there longer and not experienced it all as "sudden flashes framed in darkness," as she describes her first visions of Mexico from the confines of the diligence coach. I'm thinking particularly of nuances of expression. She'd led a sheltered life, even in those wild places she and Arthur lived, and Mexico must have offered a panorama of the new and strange.

Mary's trip to Mexico, so different from life before it and after, seems to be a watershed. If life is a narrative, Mexico was the end of a chapter, and the tougher part of the story would follow. Up to this point, Arthur and Mary had been riding on the crest of a wave. Youth, optimism, and good luck had held. But Arthur's decision to embark on an irrigation scheme in Idaho some months later changed all that.

I think of Mary in Mexico and remember the first really exotic place I ever went—Turkey in 1978. Like Mary, I'd led a sheltered life. But I'd come to England as a graduate student, so seen a bit of Europe. I remember arriving in Turkey—or do I? I suppose we flew—of course we did—from London, but I don't remember getting there. What I do remember is Istanbul: the Galata Bridge and all the merchants selling fish; the Blue Mosque; I remember old wooden houses in a run-down quarter of the old city. I remember riding in dolmuses, shared taxis crowded with strangers. I remember going south, to Antalya—now a resort, then a relatively quiet town—to Adana, to Gaziantep, Urfa, Kayseri. It seemed beyond exotic, otherworldly. I couldn't imagine I was in the same world I'd come from; that a week before, I'd walked along the cobbles of North Parade in Oxford to post a letter home saying, "Guess what? I'm going to Turkey for a month!" By the time my parents read that, I was already there, and in a pre-Internet age, I might as well have been on the moon. My untraveled parents probably felt like I was. (I've been a lot of places now, and I never really feel like that anymore—well, perhaps in Syria, a few years ago; lovely, tragic, doomed Syria, before the endless horror that has engulfed it.)

It was dreamlike. Another world. And yet, because I'd never seen anything, I wonder if I really *saw* Turkey? So many of my impressions were simply of difference, and newness, strangeness. I wish I'd written more down. Saved more. Photographs don't really tell the tale. I was younger than Mary and not looking at things with that artist's eye she had. But what I'm getting at is that sense of *otherness*. It changes you. It makes you see your old world in a new way. It reveals the strangeness in your own way of being when you realize that other lives are so different. I think the fact that Mary so immersed herself in her experiences must have made things look different when she got back.

Mary in Mexico

I'd like to ride along with her as she travels. The Mexicans are too scandalized by a woman riding, so in the towns she stays in the coach. But right now she's riding with Arthur. What does she see? What does she think?

How could I draw this? So different from anything I know. Long flat horizon today, yesterday mountains. Villages with people appearing like ghosts; women look from behind curtained—sheeted really—openings in thick-walled huts, looking, then turning away. The men stare, openmouthed, until one of the escort riders will say something, and they duck their heads like schoolboys, and turn away. Some just keep staring. Our escorts treat the peasants like beasts of burden, nothing more. Esclavos. How can they be so kind to us, yet so cruel to those people? No, it's not quite cruelty; you can't be cruel to a stone. To our jingling swordsmen, they just don't exist, these people. Is that what happens when all life is simply scratching out subsistence? But it's feudal too. I feel like I've fallen into medieval times in Italy, or Spain. I can't believe English peasants were so beaten down. What do they think of us, I wonder? Look, a woman is coming out of one of the huts. What does she want? Oh no! She is going to offer us water from a filthy dipper. I cannot! Arthur? Oh! Arthur is drinking it, thanking her in Spanish, giving her something. She is refusing. For the children, he says. She does not smile, but takes it. She turns away, glancing at me as if to say… No, gracias, no tengo sed. She looks back, like a girl. Espera! She turns, holding the dipper questioningly. Señora? A handkerchief. Nothing, but made nicely. I'm so glad I put that one in my pocket this morning. It's still starched. Por usted. She refuses. Por favor. Por favor. She accepts. She looks up at me on the horse, as far beyond her life as might be imagined. Those eyes. I will ask Arthur if we can stop so I can draw her. No? I'll remember. Tonight I'll try to remember that face. Adios. A small smile on a face not used to smiling. It looks as if it almost hurts her. This is something I would have never known.

. . .

Look from the window. Don't show your face. Here they come. The horses, huge and fierce. The soldiers! Turn away quickly! Now I can see only dust until the white-faced pair come along. A woman! On a horse. Why is she not afraid? Is she the one, for all those men? No. She is with her man, but he is not a soldier. He looks like the young priest, the one who came when Matteo died. They are slowing down, stopping. Something happening with the horses ahead. He smiles and pushes his hat back. So young! So happy. He opens his canteen and turns it up. Empty! Wait! Wait! The water bucket! Quickly, quickly! I must walk carefully not to spill. Señor? Will he accept it, from me? He looks and smiles! Gracias Señora. Señora. Not mujer. Señora. What is he reaching for? Money! No! It wasn't for that. For the children, he says. He takes my hand in both of his and presses the coin into my hand. Por favor. Gracias. And I turn to the woman. She looks at me. She says she is not thirsty. I turn. But she calls me back. A pañuelo. Not for the children. For me. She smiles. She looks at me. The horses jingle. They move on. I stand a long time watching them as they go away. The baby is crying. The money! I will buy the children cakes.

I am imagining, of course, but it might have happened. We never know the things we do that affect people. Mary might have forgotten that face, but I imagine she drew her somewhere. Maybe she used her as a model for a woman at a well that she drew for the same piece? But I see I'm mixing reality and fiction. Because I've imagined a character, she now seems to have an existence. Maybe she does?

But even there, on her great adventure, Mary is still connected to her old world, which fills her thoughts when she gets out her riding clothes, unused since Leadville:

> It may be only women who sentimentalize over their old clothes and become clairvoyant at the touch of a shabby garment, long embalmed in that subtle odor which clothing will distill from the place where it has been worn; but, even if it be purely a feminine confession, I am not ashamed to confess that memory was stronger than sight as I put on my old Colorado habit, the morning of our start, and perceived that faint, pungent smell of Indian-tanned leather, tobacco, and the smoke of wood fires. It was not

> the half-packed trunks that I saw, or the maletones, buckled ready to be slung over the mules' backs, or Ascension sweeping the damp corridor;—it was a low cabin room, with a hammock swung across the chimney corner—the blackened trails of fire-wasted pine-woods, and the long, windy reaches of the valley of the Arkansas.[13]

This sense of connection with the past, almost to the point of being unable to act in the present, is present throughout Mary's life: the sense that one *was* another person in another place; that is to say, one was someone else before life moved on and left that person behind. One wonders where that person is now? The sense of the past in the present is sometimes almost overwhelming—like when Mary "become[s] clairvoyant" at the touch and scent of an old garment worn in another place. She's not susceptible to the table-rapping sort of spiritualism that was so popular during her lifetime, but there is *something* in Mary's thinking that suggests an openness to ideas and concepts outside the absolutely conventional. Call it a highly developed intuitive quality of mind.

There is a letter, written some years later, that bears out this same quality. Mary describes waking in the night with the certainty that Arthur, who was in fact away in Mexico on another venture, was ill and needed her. It was only some weeks later that she found out that, indeed, he had been *very* ill, but was recovering. One may call such things coincidences, but openness to possibility is characteristic of Mary's thinking, and I believe it in some measure accounted for her extraordinary appreciation of the natural world. She wrote to Helena, describing the incident:

> May 18, 1893
> Last night I had one of those experiences which I have read of and thought people made up—I woke out of sleep in the early part of the night with some fear on me which I cannot describe.... This is not worry. It is like walking in the shadow of a sorrow that is coming to meet me. I lay last night for hours simply panting with dread.
>
> If Arthur is not somewhere in need of help and wanting me, or past help and to make me understand, out of the body while I am still in mine—then my nerves are giving way.
>
> Do not let anyone see this...[14]

"Do not let anyone see this," Mary says, and so I feel rather guilty, seeing it, reading it, and copying it down for others to see. But this doesn't show Mary in the light she might have imagined, as someone whose "nerves are giving way." Rather, she seems someone living life at such a pitch that she became attuned to those messages we sometimes hear, sometimes ignore, that come, who knows how, but come often enough that even the most skeptical cannot doubt that there is some process by which hearts that beat as one sometimes communicate without language or even presence. Call it intuition. Mary understood things.

So, Mexico: the drama of history and decay. It wasn't something she had much of in California, or Colorado. And she certainly wouldn't have it in Idaho, not in human or historical terms. But in all stages of her life she had a similar intensity, both of feeling and understanding. When history and culture were offered, she accepted both. When nature in all its varying aspects was what there was to be had, that was what she received and entered into, wholeheartedly. Nothing was wasted; she used her experiences in both her drawing and her fiction. The careful reader learns as much about Mary from those things as from the letters and memoirs, so that, in all, one sees Mary within the circle of her life and experience.

CHAPTER FIVE

Idaho

Over the hills where Polly and her big brother go wild-flower hunting, horses wander loose and look down from the summits, mere specks, like black mice, against the sky; they are plainly to be seen from miles away, for there is not a tree anywhere upon these hills.

—FOOTE, *Little Fig Tree Stories*

I SEE MARY up on the bluffs above her house in the canyon. She has been sketching and now she is in what used to be called a "brown study." She had written a little story called "Dream-Horses," and she is thinking about the wild horses that live high above their canyon, being born, mating, dying, all in the free open air.

It is early summer, still cool enough for Mary to wear a shawl but warm enough that she has been able to spend an hour or so alone with the landscape. The high, flat-topped bluffs across the valley are no longer surprising, but still fill her with a sense of contentment. There is something so right in this beauty that surrounds her, even though it is so unlike the world she came from. Her appreciation for it is something acquired; her vision was won by looking, by seeing, by knowing the place; by *being* there, truly immersed in that place, at that time. They have been in Idaho for several years, trying to make Arthur's irrigation scheme go. After the relative gaiety (in a manner of speaking) of Leadville, and the romance of Mexico, there was a long spell back in Milton, New York, at the family farm for Mary. There were some fruitless efforts by Arthur in various parts of the West. They lived with separation, reunion, and much uncertainty. Their second child was born.

Then Idaho.

Arthur had trouble convincing Mary of the sense of the scheme, but once convinced she became a true believer. It depended, as so many western ventures did, on eastern backing, and in this case there were even some British backers for a time. Work on the monumental project began. Mary was enthusiastic. She wrote to Helena, in a letter I have previously quoted, of her pride in Arthur's work and her hopes for his irrigation project. It is significant how committed Mary became, and how she identified, for the first time, not only with the landscape but also with the people in it. "We worship our common dream," she wrote in her letter to Helena.[1] This suggests that Mary, who for so long went along with Arthur's plans, was beginning to feel they were hers as well. Perhaps it was the grandness of Arthur's vision—for it was a grand plan, and visionary in its scope—but Mary had become deeply committed by this point, not simply in Arthur's success but to the success of the project as a whole. This is not just the artist's or author's voice; this is the personal voice, a voice of confidence and hope.

Part of the change in Mary came from the fact that they were living in an extraordinary landscape—Boise Canyon—and living in quite remarkable isolation. Boise City was ten miles away over a rough road, and though they occasionally went to town, their lives were in the canyon. I am thinking about that idea of isolation in nature, the solitude of being *in* the world, not *of* the world: immersed in a place that by its very nature could not be ignored, but had to be *known*. In this isolation, Mary came to rely more on the natural world for both inspiration and solace. When they were planning their house in the canyon, Mary wrote:

> Easter Sunday, 1885
> [The house will be on] the "second bench" back from the river and a view that it lifts one's heart up just to look at! One must get these long breaths of beauty once in a while or else die of suffocation! I find that I miss less and less the art of the world and depend more and more on this wild broad beauty that man has never touched. I did not love it so at first—At Almaden I was often very homesick and sad and felt like a prisoner far away from the world, but now—the strange intoxication of those great windy bursts of plain seen from a rise of ground that gives you miles and miles of it, with dream-like solemn processions of mountains like heroes ranged side by side in Walhalla uplifted, silent, yet in a way sympathetic and observant of the life they have left below them, grows upon me—with each absence from them and each return.[2]

One hundred and thirty-five years ago there was certainly no chance of Mary dying "of suffocation" in that remarkable canyon in which she lived, though one can imagine the isolation weighing on her. It was, and remains, a place where one can take "long breaths of beauty." And the bluffs above it give views not adequately described by "awe-inspiring." But it is a solitary place, now and then, and Mary's comment that "I find that I miss less and less the art of the world and depend more and more on this wild broad beauty that man has never touched" is her declaration of independence from her old life. I think this remarkable change got slightly lost in her letters, and perhaps even in her own thinking, because the next ten years of Mary's life, until the family moved to Grass Valley in 1895, were difficult, and sometimes desperate, despite many happy times, including the birth of Agnes, their third child.

She writes of a "strange intoxication" and "dream-like" views, comparing the mountains she sees with Norse heroes in paradise, who are "sympathetic and observant" of the life below them. This imagery is deliberate in its intention to convey the strange, overwhelming, and epiphanic qualities of her encounters with nature. The initial comparison of natural beauty with "the art of the world" suggests a return to an Edenic golden age, which is further heightened by the reference to mythological gods. And while she often references the familiar Greek gods, in this excerpt her emphasis is on the rather forbidding Norse deities, whom she paradoxically describes as "sympathetic and observant"—not one's usual impression of those stern spirits. Yet perhaps this is the right way to portray those mountains and views—forbidding, but somehow known and not feared at the same time.

After such a spiritual unfolding—and this is certainly not the only such expression of awe and wonder—one might expect some acknowledgment, comment, *something,* in response. But clearly, like her silences in response to Mary's continual requests that she come visit, Helena regarded Mary's outpourings on the wonders of the western landscape as so much *background* to her friend's life, not the substance of it. Helena responded to any practical matters Mary wrote of, and always remarked on anything to do with the children, but these outpourings of the soul, which were so important to Mary were clearly something Helena either felt unable to comment on, or unwilling. Perhaps it did not matter? Perhaps like the creation of art, Mary's expressions of the numinous grandeur she saw around her were enough in themselves and required no response. Certainly, the fact that she expressed such feelings many times, despite knowing there would be no response, gives the reader, and perhaps, who knows, Helena too, the sense that for Mary these things were primary, essential to her sense of self.

As I have suggested, Mary's long letters to Helena may have acted as a kind of safety valve to express some of the things she needed to talk about and for which she had no other audience. This is certainly true when she speaks of family troubles, worries, the children, Arthur's battles with alcohol. But these other outpourings of—what shall one call it: mystical, spiritual, numinous awareness of the world?—though spoken to Helena, were not really for Helena. I suspect Helena didn't grasp what Mary was talking about. Or if she did, she didn't feel it necessary to comment on it, which really amounts to the same thing. Although Mary loved Helena, at some level she must have known, despite her endless declarations of Helena's superiority, that in this area she *was* the Mary to Helena's Martha, listening to the sound of the divine voice, forgetting all else.[3]

By this stage in her western life, Mary really was a committed westerner. Despite her love for eastern culture, family, and friends, by this point she must have acknowledged that her life was in the West. Her sister Bessie's move to Boise with her family also must have contributed to this sense of *placed-ness*. Still, she implied, at least to Helena, that she would not stay in the West for life, writing, "Boise, you know is just what we have to do, not at all what we wish to do."[4]

One can hardly blame Mary for not wanting to be part of provincial life, considering how important her eastern identity remained to her sense of self. She did relax her boundaries somewhat when circumstances made it necessary for the family to stay in Boise with Bessie and her family for a number of months. Lots of people in Boise wanted to know her, and she did relent, particularly when she felt some eastern connection with people. I'm sure she missed a lot, through her reticence and a certain blinkered vision of western society to which she held, relentlessly, despite her feelings about the landscape and the natural world. I suspect this is because her own social triumphs, back in the heady days of the Cooper Union, when she met Helena, and the years afterward, when she knew so many artistic and literary luminaries in New York, as well as her subsequent artistic successes, were so beyond the sphere in which she had grown up as to seem almost miraculous. And her friendship with Helena became not just a friendship but a representation of a life, both lived and unlived. If she kept her friendship with Helena in the same configuration as it had been at the beginning, she could hold on to her other life. However, there were some other elements in the great friendship between Mary and Helena that bear some discussion.

Mary and Helena—A Retrospective View

Mary's youthful relationship with Helena is one with which Wallace Stegner clearly was uncomfortable in *Angle of Repose*. His squeamish skirting of an issue he felt—and clearly implied in his novel—bordered on lesbianism was both prissy and prurient. The fact is, who now cares? If two female art students spent their time wandering around in a warm glow of mutual adoration, there wasn't anything unusual in it. The nineteenth century was a good deal more relaxed than Stegner's twentieth. Both Mary and Helena went on to happy marriages. And their friendship lasted.

Carroll Smith-Rosenberg has discussed such relationships between nineteenth-century women. Clearly the relationship between Mary and Helena falls into that area of "passionate friendships" between women that the nineteenth century, for all its alleged prudishness, quite happily accepted. Smith-Rosenberg states:

> How then can we ultimately interpret these long-lived intimate female relationships and integrate them into our understanding of Victorian sexuality? Their ambivalent and romantic rhetoric presents us with an ultimate puzzle: the relationship along the spectrum of human emotions between love, sensuality, and sexuality....
>
> It is possible to speculate that in the twentieth century a number of cultural taboos evolved to cut short the homosocial ties of girlhood and to impel the emerging women of thirteen or fourteen toward heterosexual relationships. In contrast, nineteenth-century American society did not taboo close female relationships but rather recognized them as a socially viable form of human contact—and, as such, acceptable throughout a woman's life. Indeed it was not these homosocial ties that were inhibited but rather heterosexual leanings.[5]

Considering Mary's deep familial attachment to her mother and sisters, Mary's devotion to Helena is a natural progression, according to Smith-Rosenberg's argument that the intense female familial bonds that were a feature of nineteenth-century life formed a template for female friendships. She continues:

> I would further suggest that rather than seeing a gulf between the normal and the abnormal we view sexual and emotional impulses as part of a continuum or spectrum of affect gradations strongly effected by cultural norms and arrangements, a continuum influenced in part by observed and thus learned behavior. At one end of the continuum lies committed heterosexuality, at the other uncompromising homosexuality; between, a wide latitude of emotions and sexual feelings. Certain cultures and environments permit individuals a great deal of freedom in moving across this spectrum. I would like to suggest that the nineteenth century was such a cultural environment. That is, the supposedly repressive and destructive Victorian sexual ethos may have been more flexible and responsive to the needs of particular individuals than those of mid-twentieth century.[6]

Certainly, Mary never exhibits any signs of anxiety or concern regarding her relationship with Helena, and both Arthur Foote and Helena's husband, Richard Gilder, appear to have been quite contented with their marital relationships and show no signs of rancor toward their wives' "other loves," suggesting that such jealousy might be the province of a more rigidly defined masculinity than was exhibited by these nineteenth-century men. And as Smith-Rosenberg points out, male and female spheres were so widely disparate that the behavior of one's partner in relation to her own sex was a matter of little concern. After deciding to marry Arthur Foote, Mary quite openly and unembarrassedly told Helena that she had been in love with her. In a letter written in December 1873, two years before her marriage, she implores Helena, who is already married, to understand her new situation:

> December 1873
> Cannot I make you understand that the change which you speak of is not a *lessening* of my love for you, but the result of a revolution

> which must change the *nature* of *all* my relations. I did not love my Mother less when your influence was stronger with me than hers—You know, dear Helena, I *was* really in love with you—it was a passion such as I had never known till I saw you—I don't think it was the noblest way to love you—When this strange new feeling came to me, for a few months all my old landmarks swam, in a strange troubled dream about me—There is a tumult sometimes in a shallow, hill-locked mill pond (for such I am perhaps). In that tumult many things perished among others that *passion* for you, but the *love* which is in my heart for all time, you must learn by testing it—I am not *first* with you—you are not first with me—Something has come to us both which stands alone and will not be denied—but it is no more sure & lasting than the mother & sister loves, and perhaps may prove less satisfying. It is a thing I have nothing to do with—it came to me unsought while my mind was fixed upon other people & other interests—it took possession of me unawares—I would not believe in it, or realize that my world & my life were changing—I clung to the old & denied the new (in *my own heart;* this is all inside history) until at last came a sudden light and happiness—tremulous, unreal—it lasted only a day or two in the happening—but it has gone to the roots of my life—it is the same with you, is it not? It involves no destruction of the old, but a clearer, quieter, healthier love in the New Year that is before us.... Do please trust a little more in the love of
>
> Thy sister
> M. A. H.[7]

This articulation of the process of falling in love and the sea change it causes in the human heart is a beautifully succinct portrait of human emotion, revealing a depth of self-knowledge and an understanding of the complexity of Mary's feelings. The mention of Helena in relation to Mary's mother also illustrates the point made by Smith-Rosenberg, that "an intimate mother-daughter relationship lay at the heart of this female world," providing the model that other relationships with women would follow.[8]

At the Lilly Library, I read a letter from Mary's daughter, Betty, written to her in 1924, comparing the friendship of Mary and Helena to Achilles and Patroclus. I think that idealized friendship is a good way to look at it. There is something quite spiritual about the relationship that was evident to the children of these two lifelong friends.

> September 20, 1924
> I used to think the way I felt about that friendship between thee and Aunt Helena was a special glamour of my own not shared by anyone else in that large white plumes were dancing in my eyes. To thee and Aunt Helena yourselves, of course, it was friendship in a well recognized state of mind, but what it is to the daughters of that friendship is harder to define its romance and a kind of glory like that the Greeks took in their epic friendships—Achilles and Patrolclus [*sic*] etc.... Rosamund [Gilder] in her attic reading those letters and the effect of them piling upon her—it's as if I had sat beside her for years and years and felt that way too but didn't know that she did or would.... The riches thee has in thy past! Now will thee believe me about the Rems. Rosamond and I can't *both* be mad *and* Aunt Bessie. It's the most strange and beautiful life that you could imagine. Every kind of love in it—of friends and our family, then husband and children and all kinds of people and country in the basic loves yet not like anybody else's and not told as anybody else would.[9]

I suggest there is no issue with whatever the youthful relationship between Mary and Helena was. But what is important to understand is that throughout her life Mary saw herself through Helena's eyes. Almost every act, every choice, every book she wrote, every picture she drew—even when she was at the height of her not inconsiderable powers—was arbitrated by what Mary imagined Helena would say or feel. Who knows whether Helena would have been as exacting a judge as Mary was herself. But Helena became the standard by which all things were measured. And therefore, Mary kept herself in an imagined eastern world far longer than she might have otherwise done. This was Mary's way of keeping herself separate from the world around her, at least the social world, such as it was.

As I have suggested previously, I believe that part of the issue for Mary was the difference between her home in Milton and the glamorous life to which Helena introduced her. Mary had already felt a contrast between her Quaker roots and the life of literary and artistic New York where she lived as a young woman. From her homely but clearly intellectually lively life on her family's farm, she went to New York as an art student, where her "companions in those days were some of the most brilliant and fascinating young people of their time."[10] It must have been thrilling for her. And she had good friends in both Helena and Richard Gilder, who introduced her to a world to which she might otherwise not have had access. But there were clearly some difficulties for her. At one point, and after much soul-searching, she decided not to join Helena in their plan to share a studio in New York, and wrote this very revealing letter:

> September 15, 1873
> I have decided that I must stay at home next winter and I wanted to tell you this instead of writing it, because things sound so hard when they are written, and I cannot possibly tell you all the reasons in a letter. I have tormented myself about it all summer and I ought to have decided long ago. I did decide but it was against all my strongest natural leanings and it wouldnt stay. I never in my life persisted in anything that my Mother & the family didn't approve and altho' there hasn't been the least voluntary influence used to prevent my going—altho' Mother has said that she was quite willing if I thought it best, I know that she dont think it best and I cannot stand her gentle silent yielding against her own judgment.
>
> Beside, my Sister Sarah altho' she has promised & I know would be glad to do all she can to make me comfortable & happy in her home thinks that my father's house is the best place for me, Art or no Art, and you see it would not be pleasant. I dont wish you to think I am doing this alone because the family wish it. I wish it too—that is, if it comes to a choice between my family & my Art I should never hesitate for a moment as to which is first. And, after all, it may not be so bad for me as you think. I shall have the back-parlor all to myself as a studio & paint & draw in charcoal from hired models as if I were in N.Y. (and when I can go to the city now & then, I'll bring my things along and I know you will not refuse to criticize and shake me up generally.
>
> You know my stake is not as great as yours and I dont feel as if I could sacrifice my life which is a home-life to a small talent.

> You have Genius, my dear glorious girl—it compells you to do certain things which I should do deliberately, if at all, and there-in, do you see, is the difference. Your temperament leads you into one kind of life. Mine leads me into another. Why should I force myself out of my natural channel into one for which I am not fitted. The "Art Atmosphere," which you say is necessary to an artist (and of course you are right) is to me something—well, I cannot stand it! It is very intoxicating for a-while and to a certain extent stimulating, but you dont know what a reaction sets in after the strain is removed. You know last June how I went about with you & Mr Gilder and enjoyed your brilliant life and felt that it was wonderful, unreal—like something in a story—Well, my dear, it nearly used me up for the whole summer!
>
> And next winter, what with my work at the Studio, your society, which is like strong wine to me—Sarah's very strong & directly opposite influence, the journeys back & forth, my efforts to keep out of company (people are already threatening me in all directions) I should have a very wearing time. I am strong & well but people wear upon me more than I can tell you.
>
> My own people are so restful that it is a great change to leave this peaceful atmosphere for a whirl of conflicting influences & impressions. I dont think I can work when I am perplexed & excited, as I should be all winter long in one way or another.[11]

I have quoted this letter at length because it is so important for understanding Mary's finely tuned character. First, Mary says that she cannot tell Helena why she has made her decision—but puts her family's mild objections first. This tells us a good deal about Mary's own temperament, her sensitivity to the unspoken. Her family (parents and sister-in-law) are willing for Mary, then age twenty-six, to share a working art studio in New York and to live with her sister-in-law and brother, but crucially, *they don't think it is an unequivocally good idea.* That is enough for Mary. Although she loves Helena and clearly enjoys life in New York, these mild objections sway her in the direction of her own self-doubts, or perhaps simply her more modest assessment of her talents, and her own deep-seated and only then revealed inclinations. To hear her insist on Helena's greater genius, when we know what Mary did with her talents in the most adverse circumstances, smacks a little of flattery. Maybe Mary felt the need to flatter Helena to soften the blow of her eleventh-hour pullout from their plan of being two young women artists with a studio in New York. When she speaks of her "natural channel" and the difference in their temperaments, one sees that Mary knew herself very well at this stage in her life. And when she writes of her distaste for what she calls the "Art Atmosphere," one can imagine the discomfort of well-mannered, discreet, Quaker Mary Hallock among the bohemians.

Mary was also beginning to fall in love with Arthur Foote, and the intensity of Helena's way of life compared with her own "restful" people might have seemed like too potent a combination of effects. Clearly Helena de Kay was a force to be reckoned with, "like a strong wine to me," and Mary preferred life on an even keel. This may also account for the tone of this letter; Mary did not want to offend Helena, and minimizing her own talents was a way to do this. This was to be a pattern during their long correspondence: the talented, accomplished, and diligent Mary comparing herself to Helena—who gave up her own artistic practice when she married Richard Gilder—and insisting on her less significant gifts. One gets a little tired of this, and I imagine Helena, when she grew out of her slightly domineering youth, probably did too. It isn't surprising, after all, that Helena should have been used to getting her own way, being a member of New York's high society—wealthy, beautiful, intelligent, and somewhat gifted artistically. But there is nothing in Helena's later letters that encourages or acquiesces in Mary's humility; quite the reverse. Helena grew into a serious and generous older woman, devoted to her family and friends, active in civic causes, almost incidentally a socialite; while Mary became the "dean of women illustrators," a noted author, and a devoted mother and wife. Helena had felt a woman couldn't have both a career and a family; it was never a question for Mary.

Through the generosity of Indiana University, I was able to spend a week at the Lilly Library at Bloomington and read most of Helena's letters to Mary. What was I expecting? The arch figure Stegner paints in *Angle of Repose*? The idealized figure painted by Mary—better, more perfect than anyone else? I wasn't sure what I would find. So, imagine my surprise and delight when I read Helena's letters to "Molly"

("Mollykins" in their younger days) and found that like Mary's they were full of stories of children, family visits, new clothes, books, people they both knew, illness—ordinary life. But more than Mary's, Helena's letters make social comments. She was very alive to the politics of the times, and she might well have been, with her husband the editor of *Century* magazine. And she knew a lot of people. Were it not clear that these people were actually her friends, one might accuse Helena of being a bit of a name-dropper: "Harry" (Henry) James, Grover and Frances Cleveland, Emma Lazarus, E. S. Nadal, and more who are forgotten now but were the high society of New York in that gilded age. And she traveled. Her travelogues are quite interesting, if a little breathless at times. And she never stopped writing to her old friend, who went west and then drew it and wrote it as it had never been before. Mary considered herself much inferior to Helena; she was clearly awed by the circles Helena moved in, though she herself had a literary and artistic reputation far greater than Helena ever achieved. Who now remembers the name of Helena Gilder? And yet Mary Hallock Foote has been published and republished. There have been several book-length studies of her works and one biography. Her life was the thinly veiled subject of Wallace Stegner's *Angle of Repose,* which won the Pulitzer Prize largely on the strength of Mary's writings. She has been the subject of several doctoral dissertations, many essays, a play, and an opera. And now I am sitting down to add my voice to the Mary Hallock Foote industry.

Reflection

When I was at PLAYA, an artists' residency in eastern Oregon, I was in a remarkably appropriate place to think about Mary and her life. I was about 250 miles west of Boise Canyon in Idaho, in a similar topography. The nearest town with not much more than a gas pump was two hours away. So for 2017, it was quite isolated. Phone signals were bad. And there is no Internet at PLAYA except in the main lodge. The solitude possible there is remarkable. In an emergency, one could be contacted. But if there's no emergency, one is not contacted by anyone, except for the odd email, which is really more trouble than it's worth to access.

In my journal, I wrote:

I sit, looking out at vast distances, with the occasional hawk flying overhead, in this state of solitude, thinking about Mary in hers. Is this what it felt like to Mary, out there in Boise Canyon, miles from anywhere else, waiting for the irrigation ditches to be dug, the dams to be built, and the desert to flower like the Garden of Eden?

Lots of birds in this place. And now four geese wheel by my window, synchronized like swimmers; swimmers synchronized like them; wheeling by—no other word for it—in a movement musical in its grace. I hear the sound of some great harmony in the sight of their flight. Wheeling, like the wheel of the sun in the sky. It's all a wheel, isn't it? The world is now bright and yellow. Yellow and blue. I look up from typing and see the memory of a bird flying by my window. Lots of bluebirds here. Two more geese. Not as elegant as the four dancers I saw before, sailing up the sky. These ones are busy—straight across the shoreline. But I've seen them before—they greet the dawn then make a wide U-turn up near the mountain, and head back, to the wildlife sanctuary, I guess. It's about ten miles away. But this whole place is a wildlife sanctuary. Here I sit in my bird-hide watching the morning unfold, with my cup of tea, watching the show. A flock just flew up at a 75-degree angle, out of nowhere. It must be wonderful to be a bird—not one of the little fluttery ones, but one of the swooping, gliding, soaring ones. The beauty of their slow procession across the air! Gliding, slowly, with no sense of urgency. And to think, what they are doing is looking for small living things to tear apart and eat. The big beautiful ones don't eat berries and seeds. That's the small, fluttery ones. Does beauty always mean destruction? Can they be separate and still exist? Does the hawk's beauty exist apart from its savagery? Does the beauty of nature exist apart from its relentless indifference to humanity? Does the hawk know it's beautiful?

Would I be thinking these things back at my desk in London, writing about Mary Hallock Foote? What is it about vast empty spaces that sets the mind whirring on infinity? Is it infinity talking back to one? When Mary lived in these places, she tried to tell Helena about it; and Helena wrote back with stories of who she had heard singing at the opera. I'm not being critical. That's what you get in cities. Out here you get the geese, humming over the lake, on their way to where it is their instincts tell them they must go—and perhaps that is just to joy—this morning in the high places where they, and I, find ourselves.

Living in a New Landscape

I think there are stages of acclimation to solitude and absence. As Mary says, at Almaden she sometimes felt like "a prisoner"; yet arguably that landscape was more accessible and homelike than the dramatic settings in which she found herself in Idaho. Perhaps that is the point; when a landscape is completely new and does not bring up all the old remembrances of things past, it frees one to experience it in all its significance and strength. One might feel a prisoner in a landscape that looked like home, but crucially was not. The untouched "wild broad beauty" speaks to Mary in a new voice, calling her, speaking to her in a language new but already known in the heart.

The illustration *The Hill Pastures* appeared in the serialization of Mary's novel *The Chosen Valley*. The background is Boise Canyon. Can *I* get through to this scene?

I imagine she's gone high up the canyon and is looking out over the canyon to the bluffs. The details won't escape her; she'll draw this scene, or variations on it, many times. And she'll write it to Helena and use it in the novels. Can I think it? Can I imagine what might be in the mind of a woman from the East come to the West—a woman who had read Emerson's *Nature* and understood its significance? Is this what she might have thought?

What does it mean, this vast sweep of land and sky? This openness, this expanse, this empty yet full place? What's lived here? What feet trod on this grass a thousand years ago? And how is it that I am here now? And I am here now. I am more here than I've ever been in any other place. The wind, it blows right through me, and I'm part of this all.

Perhaps that's just the way I would see it. Would Mary have thought, rather, of lines of irrigation ditches, crops waving in the sun, farmers and their families, villages, towns? In theory, she would have thought of all those things and believed in the rightness of that vision, but I think the distance from the idea to its fulfillment would have protected her from the knowledge of some of the excesses of progress. And she and her family were so remote in Idaho! It's possible that the implications of progress were something she saw only through a rosy romantic vision. At PLAYA, as far from civilization as I'd ever been (except perhaps in the far outback of Australia), the world for a while didn't seem so bad. But I knew a lot of it is. And I knew that the beauty and solitude I was living in was temporary. Mary's solitude had no foreseeable ending. Arthur's projects were never fulfilled during their tenure in Idaho, and

The Hill Pastures, from serialization of *The Chosen Valley, Century,* May 1892.

a decade of their lives must have sometimes seemed wasted. But years later, in their safe haven of Grass Valley, on receiving word of the completion of a power plant that Arthur had planned and designed but never seen built, Mary wrote:

> There it was finished—the last of our dreams in Idaho, the only one to be realized then. A little thing of four stone walls planted on stone pillars sitting on a rock shelf in the riverbed, with that splendid rush of waters sweeping past and that great stretch of country far and wide—there was no stingy crowding in these pictures—they were the very land itself in its true proportions; the small but mighty work of man and the vast overpowering nature to be used and controlled.[12]

The interesting thing here is that while Mary glories in the completion of the project and suggests that nature has been "controlled," it is clear from her very language that nature has been "used" but is still "vast and overpowering." And this is something Mary knew by instinct: nature might be used, but it is the master, not the servant. Our own times tell us the same thing. We have despoiled nature, and now nature is getting its own back; the seas are rising as the planet heats up. But nature will endure, even if we do not. Around the fifth century before Christ, the Greek philosopher Protagoras said, "Man is the measure of all things." Looking out of my window at PLAYA, at a sweep of lake and sky and land like none other, I thought there was very little the measure of man had to do with it. The place was the measure of itself alone. And of such places, there is in fact no measurement. There is only a sense of wholeness, rightness.

But back to Mary: She's been walking on those bluffs. She's on her way back to the house and the children. She's been looking and thinking. Things are not going well with Arthur's never-ending, rarely succeeding plans. At one level, she is depressed; at another, she is exhilarated. Her feet touch the warm earth as she walks down the path. She stops. All her senses are open. She feels the world turning and she the still center.

What is she thinking about? Maybe some essential but ordinary thing—the children's schooling, money, Arthur's work—but maybe not. Maybe she's out there listening to the "earth's stillness." She's got some of the transcendental sense of being in nature; but she's gone beyond it. She's not just an observer; she's alive to it in the most essential way.

Mary lived in a world in which space replaced genteel notions of the picturesque. Mary's West was not picturesque. It was sometimes not even beautiful. But she was utterly alive to its meaning, and reading her descriptions makes one aware of how easy it is to ignore meaning in simple things and places. She *saw* things. Consider her trip to Mexico; she didn't miss a detail. Not one. What a life, to have been so *observant* of everything around her; to have been so *present* in her own.

I'm imagining Mary looking down at the stone house Arthur built her. She's miles and miles and years and years away from the old world she knew as a young woman. She's up there with the birds sailing high overhead. At one time she might have felt lost, but she isn't lost now; she's in the world, in the natural world, and moments like this, the inexpressible sense of being in nature, are what really keep her here. Of course, she stays for Arthur and her life, but this sense of presence in nature is something she could never truly explain, even in her letters to Helena, though she tries. She remembers what being in nature felt like

The Stone House. Courtesy of Stanford Special Collections, M0115, Mary Hallock Foote Papers, box 17.

back in Milton, the romance of the greenery-shrouded Long Pond, the lush opulence of early summer in the Hudson Valley, the evening light over long-cultivated fields, the sense of settled history of a lived-in land.

But this! It was so different as to belong to an entirely *other* set of experiences, to a different world. She feels almost dizzy looking out over the sweep of empty air from the height where she stands. If she was a bird, she could fly from this point. She closes her eyes. She feels the soar and swoop. It's not a comfort, not a joy. It is something else she feels. It is the profoundest sense of being in the world she knows. She knows that this is something she'd have never known except by living in this place, miles from anywhere, in the solitude of this land. Down below is the river, the canyon; the canyon house is just around a bend, so not quite visible; it could be a million miles away.

I can feel that hot, dry wind blowing; I can smell the grass, the dry air. I feel like I know what she's thinking, or rather, what she's not thinking. I don't think she's thinking of how much she misses the East, not anymore. I'm thinking of a line in her reminiscences, about the long hot California days, which I quoted previously: "The days are atoned for by the nights—the great nights of stars."[13]

When I was at PLAYA, writing about Mary, I wrote this in my journal:

I've just been standing on the deck of this cabin I'm staying in—like a ship at sea. And stars. Yes. A great night of stars. Have I ever seen so many stars? And to think that each one of them is the center of a solar system like this one, and there are planets, probably like this one, and someone somewhere is looking out and thinking, "I wonder if there's anyone out there?" And of course, there is. How could there not be in all that infinitude of space? How could there not be other planets with other life forms developing as we have developed—maybe more, maybe less. We can't possibly be the only ones. But the distance keeps us from knowing—will probably always keep us from knowing. So, there must be other cultures, other birds and animals, other creatures. Other life. Are they doing any better than us? Let's hope so. That's me thinking. So, what's Mary thinking on a starry, starry night, like this one, 132 years ago?

She has told us of one night before in a letter I have previously quoted:

> May 28, 1885
> I went down on the beach in the moonlight for an hour, as far from the door as the road at the foot of our yard, at home, and was instantly wrapped round with coolness and softest light and obscurity and a sound of water breaking on the "ripple" and sweeping inshore in long surges.[14]

The peacefulness of this recollection reaches out to us from the past. The intimacy of Mary's connection with the nature is emphasized by the fact that the distance to her beach in Idaho is described in comparison to her old home in New York. This immediately tells us we are in a safe and comfortable place; and she is "wrapped" rather than "surrounded" or "enclosed." She is cool, the light is soft, the water speaks in "long surges."

The experience of the starry nights in New Almaden, which she refers to when she speaks of the days being "atoned for," is like being under a vast black covering, pierced with light. The air is softer; it's not so high, and there is a promise of a morning fog to come.

As a child I lay on the roof at home, not so far from New Almaden, and looked up at the stars. The climate was similar, perhaps a little cooler where we were, but the morning fog would come just the same. And what did I see? I saw a million lights, and I knew I was looking at worlds so far away. It's the longest view we can ever get, seeing the stars, and it beats any mountain range or seascape, or volcanic park, for wonder. We'll never see anything farther away than the stars on a clear night. Mary knew that.

Mary saw nature in its benign manifestations, but she also saw it at its most terrifying. After a walk in the volcanic foothills near PLAYA, looking for petroglyphs, I thought about Mary's Idaho story "Maverick," in which the main character chooses death in the lava fields, not terribly dissimilar to the landscape I was walking in, rather than an unwanted marriage. The relentlessness of nature, its inexorability, undercuts any idea of the romance of the West in Mary's stories. There is drowning, there is death from exposure, from avalanche, from illness. Only occasionally does a bullet do for one of Mary's protagonists; usually Mother Nature pulls the trigger. This is not to suggest that Mary was not swept away, emotionally and spiritually, by the natural world. But she understood that nature, like most things, has two sides. I think of Gary Snyder's description of nature: "ferocious orderliness."[15] She wasn't drawn in by the romantic dreams that deluded so many westering pioneers. One has only to look at an illustration like *The Coming of Winter,* or *The Winter Camp—A Day's Ride from the Mail,* to understand that *she* understood.

In *The Winter Camp,* which appeared in the November 1889 issue of *Century,* one sees the reality of pioneer life. The commentary that goes with Mary's drawing tells of a trial not much considered when one thinks of the founders of the West. Her two men, and even the horse, are in a state of enforced idleness. Mary describes the plight of professional men—like Arthur—endlessly waiting for orders from above. The two men in her illustration are undoubtedly in this position. Their camp, "a day's ride from the mail," is uninspiring and shabby. The trees are bare. One man seems to be either tying a bootlace or simply staring at the ground; the other is doing some clearly nonessential task with the horse. The atmosphere is one of despondency. The makeshift chimneys lean from the roof of the makeshift home—two tents put together. Presumably their stay was planned as a temporary one—no cabins were built. But winter has come on and they are as marooned as men on a desert island. In her commentary, Mary discusses the plight of such men, comparing them to soldiers in trenches endlessly awaiting the call to action. And nature waits as well. It is clearly the dead of winter, no hope for months before or months beyond. But nature knows spring will come. These sojourners, on the other hand, may wait another spring and another summer, even another winter or more, for the call to action. Mary's text serves as a warning for those westering dreamers and undercuts the boosterism more commonly found in *Century*'s pages:

> In stories and pictures of the West we see these young men on horseback, on forced marches or exploring expeditions, engaged in exploits of love or war or money-making. A survey of the actual field of observation as regards the college graduate would find a good many of him less picturesquely employed. He is quite as likely to be found "holding down a claim" in some sun-baked valley a day's ride from the mail or comatose smelter, or wearing out the winter in an engineers' camp waiting for orders—becalmed in heart-sick idleness.[16]

Mary's message is clear, as in many other illustrations in this series: It's not all you expect. Don't get fooled by the boosters. Mary couldn't have said this directly, given *Century*'s very definite bias toward idealistic presentations of the West. But in this excerpt she manages to get the message—the fruit of her own western experience—across loud and clear, for any who might be listening.

Despite Arthur's difficulties—much like the hapless pair in Mary's illustration, he was left hanging for months and years, awaiting funding from eastern backers for his irrigation scheme—and despite her own sense of isolation, Mary found much to love in Idaho. She was profoundly affected by the landscape and was able to see beyond her own situation in it.

In a wonderful picture of Mary and Harry Tompkins, one of Arthur's engineers, in Idaho, she is a figure in a landscape that is obscure and unreadable, voiceless, to us; and yet she read it; she gave it a voice; she knew it as few have done. In a letter to Mary Austin she praises that writer for her voice in describing an equally formidable landscape: "pure woman." Mary's voice is that too. I am aware that I am characterizing

Mary Hallock Foote and Harry Tompkins. Courtesy of Stanford Special Collections, M0115, Mary Hallock Foote Papers, box 17.

women's experience of landscape as unlike men's, and that some will disagree with me. But I am trying to express that while Mary knew the landscape in its utilitarian guise, she also knew it in another less explicable, hardly expressible fashion. Looking at the figures in this picture, I want to know what they thought, how they felt, out there in that vast, visionary emptiness. I feel like I'm in a time machine looking at it: no posed Victorian set piece, it's a man and a woman on horses in among the harsh and still places of the West. Those mountains in the distance speak, but we can't know what they are saying. Except maybe she did. Can this picture tell me what I want to know about Mary's perception of the West? Am I looking downstream far enough to understand?

"Mrs. Foote, can you keep Blackie (or Trigger, or Shep) still a moment. Wiley is ready to open the shutter."

"Do you think we look properly picturesque, Mr. Wiley?" she says, laughing.

"Indeed, you do Mrs. Foote. Those mountains are as fine a backdrop as any."

"I think so too, though they're not so grand as some in Mr. Bierstadt's pictures. But they speak."

"They do. Now Wiley! That wasn't fair. I was half turned and Mrs. Foote wasn't even facing. Take another!"

"Oh it's alright Tompkins. I've got the mountains fine. It's them I was aiming for. I'll take another of you and Mrs. Foote back at the Stone House corral."

"I'm going back down now. Do you want to stay longer, Mrs. Foote?"

"Just a few minutes."

Tompkins canters away down the path.

Wiley packs up his gear. It takes some time. When he is ready to go, he mounts up on the wagon seat. "Coming, Mrs. Foote?"

"In a few minutes, Mr. Wiley. I'm thinking about a drawing. Could you wait for me at the fork?"

"Of course, Mrs. Foote."

And she waits. She sees in her mind's eye the photograph that has been taken. She wonders if the camera can see it all.

I wonder if she saw this photograph? She must have. And she must have seen the meaning in the silence of those mountains: the unspoken sense of inscrutable presence.

Could she, in her wildest imaginings, have imagined me, a hundred and thirty years later, looking at this photograph and trying to see what she saw? Probably she imagined it no more than I can imagine some other, distant woman reading my words in a century, when the world will have turned so many more corners in its inexorable and inevitable journey, and wonder how I felt, how I am feeling, trying to be in that place in the distant past.

What she sees in that slightly chilly autumnal air is the reality of the mountains; she sees their birth as the great glaciers slid away and left the valleys and canyons carved between them. She sees their creatures: hawks and eagles soaring, swooping down to grab some small thing, its paws flailing frantically as it is carried away into the sky and its end, as inevitable as our own but possibly quicker. She sees their past when nomadic people passed through on their own way somewhere less forbidding. She sees that this view has more meaning than her presence on a horse. She sees it all. She knows it, and some time she will write it. Some other time she will draw it. The wind touches her. Some small creature skitters by the horse's feet, and the horse, so well trained, dances just a little. A hawk, maybe an eagle, sweeps by overhead. She smells the iron scent of the mountain grasses; she hears the wind in the silence. The silence! The stillness of the life of the mountains. The quiet. Wiley is waiting, she knows, but she stays just a bit longer. When she looks up, the bowl of the sky seems to take her in. She feels herself disappearing into it; a sense of oneness and wholeness that she cannot express takes her. But then the horse shakes its head or whinnies. She comes back to herself, and in a moment she turns the horse toward the trail. She begins her descent. She wonders how she could ever explain this to Helena, to Arthur. She imagines Helena's slightly bemused look. "But my dear!" she would say, dark eyes laughing, "you've become a transcendentalist." Arthur though, Arthur will understand. She suddenly realizes that that is their deepest bond, besides the children—this sense of knowledge of the land.

Later, back at Stone House, Arthur is outside when she and Wiley arrive. "Do you think you'll have some good pictures for that album of yours, Wiley?" he asks. "Oh, one or two," Wiley says, turning away and leading the horses toward the barn. Then he'll go to the outbuilding where he keeps his photographic materials. He'll probably stay up all night and have the photos ready to show them by tomorrow.

Arthur looks at Mary. "Thee looks thoughtful," he says. He has a way of paying perfect attention to her when they speak. Mary comes toward him. "Arthur, up there on the ridge, I felt something I don't think I can describe."

He is absolutely attentive, silent, waiting for her to continue. She loves this in him.

"I was alone. I had sent Wiley ahead after we finished the photographs."

He is still silent, although a shadow crosses his face for a moment. He doesn't like her to ride alone, she knows. A fall, a snake, cougars, a lame horse—anything could happen. She sees this and reassures him. "I told him to wait at the fork. I was only a few minutes behind. But I needed to stay. There was something."

The shadow is gone, and Arthur is listening closely.

"Thee will think I am silly," she says, now leaning into him.

His arms go around her. "Thee? Never." He nuzzles her hair. He stands a head taller than her, and more. She fits closely into the circle of his embrace. She looks out beyond him, over his arm, freed from any self-consciousness by their closeness and the fact that she now isn't looking into those penetrating eyes of his.

"Oh, Arthur, it was as though I was taken into the sky, taken into the mountains, as though I was part of them, not myself only, but part of everything else around me, as though I was as big as the sky, and as small as the pebbles under Blackie's hooves. As though... I don't know how to say it."

He is silent. She pulls out of his embrace and looks at him. He is looking into the distance.

"Thee does think I'm silly," she says, half reproachfully, but his look takes all reproach away.

He gazes at her solemnly. "Thee understands everything. Thee doesn't need to explain."

"And thee understands it as well," she says, looking at her quiet husband with a thrill of recognition, even after nearly fifteen years of marriage. "Thee knows about it all before I tell thee."

They led their lives in nature, and these moments must have come to them more than once: that recognition of oneness that sometimes comes on us with a jolt and reminds us that we are made of the same dust as the world; we come from it, and we go back to it, and we are a part of all things. She could express it; Arthur just lived it.

I want to understand what it felt like to live so far away from where she came from, but I also want to understand that state of epiphany in nature that Mary talks about in her letters and that informs her best depictions of the natural world. She was an exile, but nature consoled her and gave her a new world, one she could live in.

Mary's fine eye saw so much. Taking his cue from Swedenborg, Emerson said that natural forms were signs of spiritual forms. While she might not, in her reticent, Quaker way, have said so much, I believe Mary probably felt it: her drawn landscapes are imbued with more than scenery. And her written landscapes give an even more revealing sense of the essential being of the natural world. I think of a passage in her late novel *Edith Bonham*, set in Idaho:

> The wind! You ceased to hear it when the train was in motion; when it stopped and you listened from your window or stood on the platform to look out, it was there—filling the silence with that breath of boundless atmosphere. It was this earth-stillness, manifest in subtle unfamiliar sounds, which gave me my first thrill—the "feeling" of the West. I have parted with it for long periods and

> half-forgotten it, but never lost it altogether. And the voice of it is that desert wind, soft, insistent, secret, that is known only in the heart of a great continent.[17]

"Earth-stillness," "the soft, insistent, secret" voice of the desert wind: this is the expression of the inexpressible. I can think of few writers, now or then, who have so adequately expressed the inexpressible experience of being in an unmodified natural world.

Mary's gift for expressing the language of the natural world was profound and came from a deep center of stillness. I would like to suggest that her habit of watching and listening to the world came, in part, from her formation as a member of the Society of Friends. Among the many good things Quakers are exhorted to do is to "set aside times of quiet for openness to the Holy Spirit...find a way into silence which allows us to deepen our awareness of the divine and to find the inward source of our strength." I want to think that's what Mary is doing. The Quaker Advices also tell the followers to "Rejoice in the splendor of God's continuing creation," and I think she's doing that too.[18] I wish I could talk to her, but since I can't, her books can talk to me.

Mary's understanding of nature was often seen in her story lines; and her characters reflect Mary's own understanding. This is especially true in *Edith Bonham.* In this novel, she has given to Edith, based on her friend Helena, her own deepest feelings. Mary would have loved to have shared the West with Helena. Inexplicably, although she was a constant traveler, Helena never came west despite repeated invitations. So, *Edith Bonham* is wish-fulfillment in many ways, none more so than this attribution to Helena of a kind of deep sensibility and awareness that was, as far as evidence can reveal at this distance, Mary's alone. At one point in the novel, Edith says:

> We were in the very heart of the morning light moving swiftly across the grey-green plain. The line of the mesa-lands, low at first with mountains snow-capped above it, now rose brown and bare (where ploughed ground had gone back to desert) close ahead and cut off the mountains.[19]

"The very heart of the morning light": we're there. Mary has saved that moment from a hundred years ago and given it back to us. The mesa speaks to Edith as the desert has spoken to seekers before. Her six weeks on the mesa is just a little more than forty days in the desert. Later she reflects:

> Alone I could stand and open my chest with great breaths of that air, and clasp my hands behind my head and look up deep into that amazing sky! Early morning, and evening after Douglas went away, I chose my time. Each morning the mountains were there inconceivably the same. The Owyhees swung down along the southern sky where they approached the Boisé Mountains with their near foothills, there was a break and through it one looked far off into the Powder River country and saw the Blue Mountains of Oregon. As I knew very little Western geography these names were as new to me as names in a fairy-tale. All fairy-tales—except one—were tame to this. "And the evening and the morning were the sixth day," I used to say to myself aloud. I fancied I knew why evening came before the morning in that stupendous record. Night is the constructive time when miracles are to be wrought; night for the mind and spirit, day for the body and will.[20]

In this passage one sees Edith choosing her time for this spiritual communion. She must be alone for the experience, for such heightened awareness comes only in solitude. "The mountains were there inconceivably the same"—inconceivable because of their dreamlike quality. But the mountains are in motion: they "swung down along the southern sky" and "approached the Boisé Mountains." One feels the living quality of the landscape in Edith's thoughts and the sentience accorded to nature. One understands what it is to be the still center while the world moves around one. She looks off into unimaginable distances—Blue Mountains, Powder River Country—magical, more than magical. As she says, all fairy tales "were tame" except one. Edith is seeing Creation.

I feel certain that this passage is not a literary construct; that here we have Mary's authentic voice, telling us what this scene meant to her and giving us this moment of epiphany in nature.

In her reminiscences, Mary talks about being in their place in Boise Canyon:

> And now autumn had given warning. The wild geese were flying south; the sun set earlier in the brooding intensity of color and a longer, more marvelous afterglow followed calling us all out of the house to watch it deepen and flood the world above us. It was a three-story place: the river and the beach floor, the hill where we said we should build if that ever came to pass, and the bluffs that rose to the level of the mountain pastures. Twilight sank first upon the river floor; the dark fronts of the bluffs took strange colors scored by shadows like the sculptured doorways of Petra, rock city of the desert. The shadow mounted, the rose-pink turned purple and greenish and died out.[21]

The powers of observation here are the artist's, but also there is a sense, once again, of historicizing, placing their canyon among ancient places, recognizing its geographical antiquity. Petra, where Mary had never been and never would be, is an apt comparison to the walls of her rocky canyon in Idaho, did she but know it. I have been to both places, and there is indeed something of the same atmosphere in them—high and wide, full of light and distance.

As in so many of Mary's observations, there is a sense that nature *knows* something that we do not; that it is the canvas on which our lives are painted, and which will be painted over with other lives when we are gone. Writing of 1886, a year when, due to her pregnancy, she was confined to the canyon for several months before and after the birth of baby Agnes, she said:

> And every day and all day the wood doves up the gulch were calling, calling, hid in the willow thickets. [Here follows a list of friends and family dead.]...The air was heavenly, soft and sweet, wild roses scented every breath of wind from up the gulch and all day the patient, maddening doves kept saying something we could not get out of our heads and could not understand.[22]

The use of nature as a template for understanding is not simply the pathetic fallacy writ large; rather, it is an acknowledgment of a continuity between ourselves and nature, a realization that we do not exist except as we exist in nature. This passage, with its haunting imagery—one can hear the doves, one can smell the air and the roses—tells us that as our lives pass, nature continues in its changeless rhythm.

Earlier in the reminiscences, this sense that nature speaks to us is made explicit in Mary's description of her arrival in Idaho at Kuna:

> But what a morning! Meadow larks were springing up all about us—it was April and we knew there were nests and wildflowers hid in the sage beneath those jets of song.
>
> ...Their note was a brief song, sad and sweet, that rained down to us from the sky. It haunted us, that song, every spring of all our years in Idaho, as it welcomed us that April morning. The birds and the wind filled the vast brooding silence—*the desert wind that talks, that whispers, that brings messages from the infinite filled with whatever each human soul that listens can put into it.* (my emphasis)[23]

Here again there is the sense that nature has something to say to us, *if we will listen.* There is a language we may learn, if we try, or perhaps if we are given the gift.

The poetry of Mary's life never escaped her, despite many trials. The value of the "beautiful times" was always evident. She tried to express these in her letters to Helena, possibly aware that Helena pitied her western life. But mainly, she wanted Helena to understand the beauty around her. "Yet we have had some beautiful times here, strange and poetic; if only we could have distinctly seen the end of it and the way out."[24] Her understanding that beauty and poetry and strangeness might be linked makes her sound strangely modern, even postmodern, for a Victorian lady.

Mirror Images

In one of her letters from Idaho, Mary describes a photograph she is sending Helena, and in an extraordinary piece of luck I came across the very photo in an album in the archives at Stanford Special Collections.

> June 6, 1885
> Please to note the group of three on horseback. Arthur is on the

> right in the helmet hat, Mr. Tompkins in the middle on a white nosed horse ("Blue Pete"), Mr. Keyser (the young gentleman from Baltimore) on the left in a broad Panama hat and a straight profile— The figures are small but we think very characteristic. The background is that little "draw" between the hills where the brook comes down in the midst of a tangle of willows and wild roses, where we hear the wood doves fluting at sunset or in the early morning— Wherever the hills part you see more hills beyond—and when you climb up one, the widening horizon gives you a hundred more— That is looking towards the West, where the mountain pastures extend for ninety miles, forming the foot hills of the Bitterroot Mountains—Towards the river it is all broken up by the chain of lava bluffs and the river's winding channel. The color is sober but not melancholy—I used to pine for green fields that first summer in California, but I have grown to love these soft low monotones, that give such importance to a bit of human life and color, and with such splendor of skies and of atmosphere and radiant distances, like gates of an earthly paradise.[25]

But perhaps even more interesting than comparing the picture to its description is comparing the picture to an illustration for Mary's novel *The Chosen Valley,* in which the middle figure in the photograph becomes the main figure in a scene in which he is looking backward toward a settlement while moving forward through the landscape. The image is so similar, I wonder if Mary used a camera lucida.

This description is specific and deeply appreciative, seeing what is beyond the surface, going from the details of the "little 'draw'" and the "tangle of willows and wild roses" to the "widening horizon" and "a hundred more" views, then the geologic details, and finally the personal reflection on color—she was ever the artist—and finally a crescendo of high-flown metaphors. But it works, beautifully. We see those radiant distances, the splendid skies, the earthly paradise; not perhaps in the photograph, but her drawing certainly carries the weight of the prose. She *saw* all that in the photograph, and then communicated it in her letter and the drawing.

In Mary's drawing the man on the horse is giving a backward glance at what looks like a campsite and the valley. I wonder what the story of this is—what was in her head when she chose that figure from the

Three horsemen. Courtesy of Stanford Special Collections, M0115, Mary Hallock Foote Papers, box 17.

photograph to become the central figure in her drawing? What did she imagine when she drew this man looking back: ruefully? hopefully? His posture doesn't suggest anger or despair. Rodman Paul uses this picture as the frontispiece to Book V of *A Victorian Gentlewoman of the Far West,* "The Endurance Test." It would be nice to know if Mary thought of using it, but there's nothing in the manuscript to give a clue. I rather think not. But it gives us another reading of the picture.

Idaho was really the fulcrum of their western life. Arthur's troubled irrigation scheme nearly broke both of them. But imagine her life: making a home there, despite it all!

> June 1888
> There is nothing that will ever quite take its place! Dreamers we are, dreamers we always will be, and what is folly and vain imaginings to some people is the stuff our daily lives are made of—And there are thousands like us! If there never had been, there would be no great West. We may not be the ones who succeed, but to every one who dreams and realizes his dreams there must be a hundred or a thousand who dream and fail. I don't mean to say it is a good thing, but it is a thing that always will be true, and may as well be

"Dolly was serving a housekeeper's apprenticeship."
From *The Chosen Valley, Century,* September 1892.

accepted, as a part of real life even in America and today. None of the people out here are "realistic." They are all idiots of one kind or another! You should hear the stories we hear—[26]

One gets the sense Mary is trying to make the West comprehensible to Helena in this letter, but also that she herself is farther and farther away from that person she once was, who came West with such a lot of preconceived ideas. And in the following letter, there is a bit of (justifiable!) bragging of her adventurousness:

August 30, 1884
The young men slept in the barn and Arthur & I had a bed made for us with clean sheets and bedding of patchwork—in the open air—just plain under the sky. I didn't sleep much for the stars—such a multitude of them, over head, and so inquisitive—and the cattle

in the corral, sighing and taking deep breaths—and dogs barking and far off the yelp of a cayote [*sic*].

I make a great many words about a small adventure. But I love to see strange places and to do the unexpected thing.[27]

This "small adventure" of Mary's seems to me like one of life's perfect moments. One wonders how Helena, living in fashionable Manhattan responded to it?

Although Mary's life was not easy, it was full of joy and remarkable moments, like this one, from her reminiscences, in which she describes the day of her youngest child's birth:

> The day had been stifling hot with showers around us on the mountains cutting off our down-cañon wind. The baby came at sunset, and out of the window of my room, they told me, a double rainbow could be seen spanning the hills where the river enters the cañon. A sight so beautiful that he who did not know that he had another daughter about two minutes old, came to the door and begged them not to let me miss this welcome to our Cañon baby. I laughed to think of it afterwards—how Bessie held the door against him and said sternly, "She is not thinking of "rainbows"![28]

In 1909, years after they left Idaho, Arthur's irrigation project was completed under the hand of a man who had been one of his junior engineers. It must have given some satisfaction to them both to have had this acknowledgment of Arthur's role in that project:

> Most highly honored—most revered—are those who, as the years pass, are found to have stood on elevations during their day from which they commanded a horizon far beyond the sight or understanding of the masses of the people. We know not what we owe them.... A quarter of a century ago Mr. Foote saw these possibilities which we now so fully realize....
>
> It would be impossible to even briefly refer to every project suggested by Mr. Foote which has become an actuality.
>
> D. W. ROSS, Idaho State Reclamation Engineer[29]

Wouldn't they have been surprised to know that now there is a splendid memorial and park at the site of their old house in the canyon; that there is a Mary Hallock Foote Day celebrated in Boise annually; that there are still writers reading her words and thinking about her life; that she is discussed at academic conferences; that her books are republished; that there are two biographies and one book-length study of her works, a novelization of her life story, an opera, a play about that novelization and its excesses, as well as many essays and articles and doctoral theses. And now this book, nearly a century after her last novel was published! I so wish they could have seen Arthur's dream fulfilled: all that water.

In conclusion, I suggest that one of the most remarkable things about Mary Hallock Foote, which became apparent during the Idaho years, was that she looked at the landscape in a new way, at least a new way for American writers of her generation. Something akin to that of transcendentalism, her view was broader. I have argued that that view had more in common with that of the ancient Greeks than with any modern tradition. Like the ancients, she expressed reverence and awe, certainly, but also love on a very personal level, which may seem strange considering the place to which she had come. Her old world encompassed land that could be understood in terms of farming, making, growing, even mining. Idaho was different. That a Victorian lady, used to cities, villages, and much lived in farmland, used to a world controlled by humanity, should so readily embrace the nonhuman, even *inhuman* grandeur of the wide western spaces in which she found herself is telling. Her eyes were open; her ears attuned themselves to the vast stillness; she drank the waters of silence and lived in a world of earth, stone, water, and stars. I believe she was open to the spiritual experience of the land and that this is revealed in her writing: listening to the silence for the sound of the spirit.

CHAPTER SIX

Grass Valley

MARY AND ARTHUR moved to Grass Valley, California, in 1895, and remained there until 1932 when they moved East to live with their daughter, Betty. Although the Idaho years were behind them, that time continued to inform Mary's thinking and writing, particularly in her novel *Edith Bonham,* written after her lifelong friend, Helena, died.

The Grass Valley years were the first period of financial security for the Footes, and while Mary sometimes spoke of herself as "old" in letters to Helena, she was only forty-eight when they arrived, for the second time, to live in California. Mary also talked about being finished with writing. In a letter sent to Richard Gilder, she says:

> July 9, 1896
> We are not very proud. We don't expect to have the earth: and this little corner of it is quite enough to content us. And I can rest my stupid head which is no good anymore. Witness the poor stuff I sent to Mr. Johnson.... When one loses the power of self-criticism one had better stop.[1]

And yet some of her best work was to come—*The Desert and the Sown, The Valley Road, Edith Bonham,* and *The Ground Swell,* as well as two well-researched historical novels, several short stories, and her memoirs! Mary so often exhibits this lack of self-belief, and yet she must have known how really accomplished she was. It seems to go hand in hand with her constant assertions of Helena's superiority, in all ways, to her. Is this also a product of her upbringing? Or perhaps simply her character?

The terrible irony of their life in Grass Valley, with all its comforts and successes, is that it was there, eight years after they arrived, in 1904, that the fatally defining moment in Mary and Arthur's lives occurred. Their beloved daughter Agnes died of complications of appendicitis at

Agnes, aged about ten, and Mary, circa 1874. Courtesy of the Lilly Library, Indiana University, Bloomington, the Gilder manuscript collection, box 24.

the age of seventeen. This tragedy almost silenced Mary for six years and affected her throughout the rest of her long life. Although she lived for another thirty-four years, Mary ends her memoir with the death of Agnes, which happened when she was fifty-seven years old. Darlis Miller writes:

> Reflecting on her "one great sorrow" nearly six years after her child had died, Molly said it "remains an extra heart-beat big and heavy that throbs once and sinks again like a great wave striking the shore that comes from far away. It is sure to come again." But life did go on; Molly coped with routine household matters and found solace in her family.[2]

Mary did not write significantly for several years after Agnes's death, except correspondence, and even that was limited. When she did pick up her pen again, she wrote, in rapid succession, two historical novels, *The Royal Americans* and *A Picked Company,* followed by *The Valley Road,* the story of a family involved in a mining and irrigation project, with the backdrop of the San Francisco earthquake of 1906. When Helena died in 1916, Mary was devastated, but by 1917 she had written and published *Edith Bonham,* the eponymous title character based on Helena. Set in Idaho, elegiac in tone, the novel incorporates many of her own Idaho experiences.

Mary's final novel, *The Ground Swell,* published when she was seventy-two, is considered by many to be her finest. Dealing with issues of family relations, war, and death, in this novel Mary finally comes to terms with modern women through the character of Katherine Cope, the doomed youngest daughter of an older couple. The tragic death of Katherine, who dies while nursing wounded soldiers in France during World War I, echoes the death of Agnes fifteen years previously. "A mother's thoughts at my age are so often a review of her own mistakes with her children," the protagonist Lucy Cope says, and one hears the voice of the author.[3] This novel rings true on so many levels and is a fitting final work in Mary's long and productive career.

MARY AND *ANGLE OF REPOSE*

Mary worked on her reminiscences until about 1925, and thereafter tried to find a publisher for the book, with no success. Edited by Rodman Paul and published as *A Victorian Gentlewoman in the Far West* (Mary's original title was to have been *Background with Figures*), the work finally came out in 1972, published by the Huntington Library, a year after Wallace Stegner's *Angle of Repose.* As previously noted, the similarities are extraordinary, as is Stegner's use of Mary's letters and much of the text from the original reminiscences, strangely unattributed.

I confess that at this point I find myself asking, as one dampening acquaintance did, why am I doing this? While I do find Mary endlessly interesting, in her fiction, journalism, and her letters; and while I find it significant that she gave the female perspective in western art for the first time; others have written about her and written very well. What am I saying that has not been said already, and better? Critically, how is this work any different from what Stegner did, appropriating Mary's life for his own ends? I keep asking: If Stegner had not "warped" Mary's story, would there be any point in what I am trying to do? If he'd used quotation marks where required and told the truth? But he didn't, and he changed her into just enough of a coquette to make the rest of it untrue. And he turned dear, financially reckless but endlessly loving and loyal Arthur into a kind of monster. Young Arthur became little more than a silent cipher, and the clearly lovely Betty Foote became a nonentity. And much, much the worst thing Stegner did was to use darling, whimsical, tragic Agnes as a convenient plot vehicle for his story, ignoring the fact that her name, and character, belonged to a much loved, very real person. The fact that he used her actual name in the novel is inexplicable, except as a sign of how minimal he considered Mary's own literary reputation and legacy and her reality as an actual person, making her simply grist for his literary mill. And Helena, whose letters tell an entirely different story than Stegner's, becomes the rather contemptible, haughty Augusta, possibly the biggest villain of the novel, combining in one character the three things that clearly threatened Stegner most: accomplished women, the eastern establishment, and natural refinement.

None of this would matter if *Angle of Repose* were a novel whose characters are not readily identifiable, though the appropriation of Mary's letters and memoirs would rankle. But it does matter. Mary deserves better than to be remembered as the "Susan Burling Ward" of Stegner's novel.

But again, Stegner's treatment of Mary's works is a side note. Apologists for him argue that it was NOT plagiarism to lift whole pages of the letters and reminiscences without proper attribution. Nor was it wrong to create a character who was clearly and recognizably Mary Hallock Foote (using only slightly altered names—in most cases Foote and Hallock family names, which made the renaming even more obvious), and to use the life of this remarkable woman to make *his* name and reputation. *Angle of Repose* stands on the shoulders of all of Stegner's other novels. This is entirely due to the fact that *it* stands on the shoulders of Mary Hallock Foote, through Stegner's unattributed use of her letters and reminiscences. There is no other way to express this unpalatable truth. Stegner was good at many things, but he was not a great novelist. *Angle of Repose* is a great novel, but the greatness is not Stegner's to claim. How impotent his remarks sounded when he became aware that Mary's reminiscences were to be published a few months after *Angle of Repose*. In a letter to Janet Micoleau, Mary's granddaughter, the family member who gave Stegner access to the letters and reminiscences, he states that he has used "[a] paragraph at a time at the most."[4] Even the most casual reader of both the reminiscences and *Angle of Repose* can see more, much more than that, lifted directly. (To the naysayers, I say simply, read the books side by side. Read Mary's first, then read Stegner. Be prepared to be shocked.) And for a scholar of Mary's letters, the unacknowledged and freewheeling borrowing of them is deeply disturbing. One reviewer in the *Atlantic* praised Stegner's narrative voice in the novel, referring to the letters between "Susan" and "Augusta"—Mary and Helena. Referring to the device Stegner uses of his main character, Susan/Mary's grandson, speaking into a tape recorder, William Abrahams wrote:

> Gradually other voices are heard on the tape: Susan's, in particular, in letters that are a triumph of verisimilitude, perfectly matched to Mr. Stegner's carefully rendered locales and social discriminations. As she and Oliver come into clearer focus—she perhaps the more vulnerable, but finally the more fascinating and memorable of the two—and as more and more of their extraordinary experience is brought into the foreground, the device of the recorder is discreetly modulated: for long stretches nothing is allowed to break the communication that has been established.[5]

"The communication" Abrahams refers to is nothing more than the lifting of text from Mary's own letters and memoirs. Reading this, one wonders how Stegner could have not felt some guilt or shame. Yet even after receiving this undeserved praise, Stegner did not issue an apology or even an admission. Was it simply that he thought Mary's life and work were fair game—there for the taking—like the "virgin land" was to the first settlers? We will never know. But I am grateful to Stegner for one thing; he brought me to Mary Hallock Foote's works, as he did many others. Still, he seemed not to know her as more than the simple "eastern woman goes west to civilize the wilderness." None of his other novels has a female character in it remotely like *Angle of Repose*'s Susan Burling Ward. And this is primarily because Susan *is* Mary, whatever denials Stegner chose to make. The language is Mary's, the descriptions are hers, the plot line is hers—everything. It has been estimated that more than 20 percent of *Angle of Repose* is actually Mary's own words. Much more is simply paraphrased. But again, Stegner is a minor actor in this play. Let us finally leave him and this ugly controversy and return to the really important character.

Resolution

I'd like to return to Grass Valley, where Mary spent the next thirty-seven years of her long life. Mary ends her reminiscences with Agnes's death in 1904, only briefly referring to the following years. If Mary worked on the memoirs until roughly 1924, that is twenty years condensed into a page and a half. With characteristic modesty, she does not speak of the five novels written in the intervening years. More surprisingly, she does not mention Helena's death in 1916:

> All that has happened here since would be too difficult to tell for one so deeply implicated through her relations to the chief actors, yet so powerless, as myself. The next generation took the lead in household and mining affairs and made their own decisions, as we made ours; though never did I achieve that extraordinary self-effacement which ruled my own parents when their children's problems called for action.[6]

She speaks of "the magic perspectives of memory—it keeps what we loved and alters the relative size and value of many things we did not love enough."[7] So, for whatever reason, Mary leaves twenty years or so of her life out of her last book, though there are some clearly autobiographical details in both *The Valley Road* and *The Ground Swell.* (After 1924 her writing was mainly letters to her family. Though many of these letters are still in the possession of Mary's descendants, they are sadly illegible except to those for whom they were intended, now long gone.)[8]

And yet somehow, this seems right. Mary's reminiscences are the memories of their life in the West: successes and failures, triumph and tragedy, the birth and growing up of her children, and the loss of one. The years in Grass Valley, while eventful, were not full of the drama of movement, great hopes, and great losses. Grass Valley was a quiet harbor, at long last. Even Odysseus found Ithaca in the end.

In a very fortuitous moment, I came across one of Helena's letters to Mary, with its reply, at the Lilly Library. It is worth looking at the two together to see something of their friendship. The letters were written shortly before the move to Grass Valley, when the Footes' future was still uncertain. The first excerpt is Helena to Mary:

> January 13, 1895
> Your letters, the last two, fill me with unrest—I know you so well, I think I know your needs & I do not see the way clear at all. First

> & foremost—if you *could & would* come to me for three or four or six months, you should have a good bright pretty room to sleep & work in & a latch key—& such a welcome!![9]

The letter goes on to suggest that Mary might try her hand at depicting the life of New York:

> New York is an untouched field. . . . If you should decide to come, you know how happy we should be, & you cannot tell what there might be for *me* in it—as we can never measure what our force is with others.[10]

Despite the genuineness of Helena's invitation and concern, this is Mary's reply:

> January 20, 1895
> As for your invitation to come and stay with you, and your thought of the children too—well, such invitations are out of fashion these days—even between blood sisters—I am touched more than I can say at your extravagant goodness to me: and if I loved New York and its joys and inspirations (and I *do* love them)—if I loved that kind of thing more than I love you, and prized it more than I prize the delicate strength and poise of a friendship too rare to be tampered with—why I daresay I should come—and make you sick and weary of me.
>
> No, dearest girl, if there is a possession of mine that I am jealous for and about, it is your love for me. I would not, for all the worlds there are, "work it for all it is worth," in advantages, social & what not. No, I'm not coming, bag and baggage, scrip & scrippage or either with, or without, my children, to make your love a means of this and that advantage to me; or to my work: It is like you to expect it—and I love the invitation and feel the richer for it; but I want, if possible, to keep these grim stupid chapters of my life to myself; they are meant for me, or I shouldn't have them—and I'm not going to wiggle out of them, but take the experience *straight*. But I can't help the weakness of crying out sometimes, and confessing to you that I am tired and that the pasture for mind and spirit is getting pretty short.[11]

I like the final farming metaphor with the picture it gives of Mary as part of the natural world. As much as she did miss New York, as she says, with its "joys and inspirations," she was utterly embedded in nature. But what seems to me most significant in this letter is the fact that beyond the wish, quite understandable, not to upset the balance of a friendship by making Helena "sick and weary" of her is the sense that her troubles are "meant for me, or I shouldn't have them." This belief in the inevitability of suffering and its benefit seems less Quaker than Calvinist, but might also be seen simply as a typically stoical, female response to life. She bears a lot, perhaps too willingly, but it is hard to imagine how it might have been otherwise unless Arthur had been a different man and she a different woman.

But this spirit of resignation has its positive side, as seen in another letter written later in the same year, when the Footes had moved to Grass Valley and life was looking up:

> December 17, 1895
> I read in the back of The Century (somebody's aphorism) that we make character more through what we relinquish than through what we acquire.... This, I truly think, will be my last disappointment in the way of our affairs:—last because I never will let myself expect anything again. Dreams are very well: but dreamers have to pay for their dreams. I have said more now than I meant to. Let it perish like the dream itself.
>
> May all blessings gather to your midst: this happy season. We shall be happy too, because we *are* happy, in spite of the Deuced Luck, or ill-luck, which must have some reason for following us. We may as well make friends with it.[12]

This resignation and acceptance of their troubles (which were probably inevitable, given the complexity and attendant corruption in the mining and irrigation industries in the nineteenth century, and their dependence on the caprices and whims of eastern backers), without the need to seek blame or justify, reveals again the fineness of Mary's character. She bore so much without losing an inch of her goodness and positivity, though she does admit to being "tired."

One sees the same kind of acceptance, though in a different key, in the nineteenth-century thinker Maurice Maeterlinck, now mostly forgotten. I came upon the following quotation in a book that belonged to my grandmother. She was a generation younger than Mary, but was the same kind of persevering, long-suffering western woman. She too had married a man who was set to make his way in the West. My grandparents were from Wisconsin, and my grandmother had been to university and studied to become a teacher, although I do not know if she ever spent time in a classroom. She was clearly of a philosophical turn of mind, if her library is anything to go on. My grandfather started at the bottom in the logging industry and worked his way up to become manager of the Canadian operations of one of the large western timber companies. But when they were young, he and my grandmother were often separated when he went away for long periods as a "timber cruiser." My grandmother did stay with him on these excursions when she could. So perhaps this little volume of Maeterlinck that I'm holding in my hand was held in hers, read in some remote timber camp back in the early 1900s.

> Let us remember that nothing befalls us that is not of the nature of ourselves. There comes no adventure but wears to our soul the shape of our everyday thoughts; and deeds of heroism are but offered to those who, for many long years, have been heroes in obscurity and silence. And whether you climb up the mountain or go down the hill to the valley, whether you journey to the end of the world or merely walk round your house, none but yourself shall you meet on the highway of fate.[13]

Wisdom, perseverance, and self-knowledge: the nineteenth century was good at all three. Mary was particularly good at all of them!

The first few months of their stay in Grass Valley was uncertain. James Hague, Arthur's brother-in-law and the owner of the North Star Mine, took some time to finally settle on giving Arthur a permanent position. Mary wrote to Helena:

> North Star Mine, March 22, 1896
> The first soft spring nights are here; I take my usual evening tramps on the usual western "quarter deck" high above the usual wide

> dim valley; but this time there are trees in the depths of the valley, and great pines brooding over our cottage roof. The same pursuing sense of insecurity is here too, but I cannot imagine life without that.[14]

But soon all was settled and the Footes were Californians again, and would remain so for the next thirty-seven years. It makes one quite happy to see Mary settled after all her roaming. She was never meant for a gypsy life.

> North Star Cottage, December 6, 1896
> I have never been in any one place that seemed to me so home-like—so like a place to ask one's dearest friends to come. In Boise I never felt like myself. In the Cañon all was provisional, and alas, so morbidly unreal. This is the sort of thing that could last.[15]

Mary's letters from Grass Valley are more and more concerned with her growing family. She continued writing, but as she says, the children came first for her. Additionally, Mary did not need to earn as she had in Idaho, so the pressure was not so great.

> December 22, 1897
> Well; it is middle-age here with us. The time for planning & organizing the children's lives—the choosing of schools, which decides the choice of friendships, on which perhaps marriage—the whole future of a fraction of the race—depends! It is more than the making of books & pictures. They can wait, forever, if need be! We are our children's destiny, at this period—Later we fall off like the seed-pod, after its work is done—[16]

Mary doesn't write much about nature in Grass Valley, though they were living in the midst of it. Like New Almaden, the setting was beautiful, but not awe-inspiring as Idaho and Colorado had been.

In 1901, she wrote, "Softly: we are perilously happy this year. Somehow I don't know why. It's dangerous to be happy at our age, with three hostages at large."[17] This seems so horribly prescient, with the death of Agnes three years away. Mary's letters to Helena, after it happened, are unbearably moving:

> May 18, 1904
> Now the experiments in "Education" are over. *Our* education will begin now.
>
> There is much to regret. It is more a passion of love, fearing it did not express itself fully enough while yet there was time.

> October 23, 1904
> I cannot say that things grow easier very much.
>
> If we parents were alone with our losses; but the devastation this has wrought in my poor lost girl's life. I must not talk of it, even to you.[18]

Mary lived in an age better acquainted with early deaths than ours is; I do not think that made them any easier to bear.

After the tragedy of Agnes's death in 1904, Mary did not write professionally again till 1910. But life went on, as it inevitably does despite heartbreak. The San Francisco earthquake of 1906 appears in Mary's letters, and later, when she begins to write again, it appears as the background of her 1915 novel, *The Valley Road.* The Foote's daughter, Betty, was married to Tod Swift in 1907, and soon gave birth to a baby daughter, who was named Agnes after her aunt, which made Mary very happy. But the little family made the decision to move to Massachusetts for Tod's work in 1910. This was a huge blow to Mary. As ever, she wrote to Helena.

> June 10, 1910
> The house will be haunted when they go.... But I say to myself, over and over.... *This* can be borne—this separation—because of the messages and knowing where they are and that they are happy.
>
> Yet it is as total as the others. The house is just as empty. The thoughts just as full.[19]

Mary had begun writing again, and her first historical novel, *The Royal Americans,* came out in 1910. Since Agnes's death she had written very little, except for a dark short story, "Gideon's Knock," written in response to an appeal after the San Francisco earthquake.[20] *The Royal Americans* was an unusual book, dealing with a group rarely used for novelistic purposes, American colonists who sympathized with the British during the Revolutionary War. It is set partly in the Hudson Valley, which Mary knew so well, and I wonder if it was a comfort to her to go back to those well-remembered childhood scenes, in an age far from her own.

Although Mary essentially ends her memoirs with the death of Agnes, there is enough biographical material in *The Valley Road,* which has as its center the San Francisco earthquake and evacuation, and *The Ground Swell,* which has as its main setting Pescadero Beach, where the Footes had several summer camping holidays, to get a fair idea of what the Footes' later years in Grass Valley were like.

After Helena died, Mary wrote to Helena's children.

> To Rodman Gilder
> June 16, 1916
> My heart is not broken, it is heavy with the treasure of our past.
>
> To Rosamund or Rodman Gilder [illegible]
> August 22, 1919
> Last night was a warm soft windy night, the tide coming in and all the doors and windows upstairs open to the sounds outside.... I thought of your mother reading aloud to me in the old parlor at Milton, kept cool with shutters barred against the sun of one of our hot June days; she in thin muslin with bare throat and elbow sleeves sitting on the old black horsehair sofa, her beautiful voice and pronunciation, and she was either reading aloud, or repeating to me from memory part of a German poem, a "lyric" that begins with the sound of water—the rush up the sand and the soft sigh as the wave subsides... what was the poem? What were the words?...
>
> Sound of all sounds on earth most loved by me.[21]

"What was the poem? What were the words?" The answers to these questions are lost, as is so much of what we might know about Mary, but so much remains, if we listen.

Agnes died in 1904. Helena died in 1916. Mary could never fully recover from these two blows. But she lived in Grass Valley many more years, until 1932. I imagine her walking in the woods near North Star House, thinking over her long life. She had had losses, terrible ones, but she still had a daughter and a son, grandchildren, Arthur, and, crucially, she had nature. I can imagine her in the Northern California woods.

The flowers are beginning early. But these California wildflowers always come early. It will be another month before the flowers come up in Milton. So strange to think of people living in the old house. Not us. Not Quaker Hallocks. That's what they called us. No harm meant. Twenty years now since Agnes died. I remember how she used to play "primitive woman" in these woods. How she loved it! What a funny, darling she was. She would be thirty-seven. Thirty-seven! With children of her own. Maybe living nearby. No, I mustn't even think about that. And eight years since Helena...Helena. If only she had come West, just once. I wonder why. I'll always wonder. These trees—they've been here how long? Long before us. Indians probably passed under them. What tribes were here? Arthur will remember. Here's the clearing I like, with the long view. All trees. Rolling away for miles. The view in Idaho was different—so different! Wide and high and empty and full of the sky. Life was so hard, and so beautiful. And Leadville! What we could see there! Mountains and mountains after mountains. And there was Santa Cruz and the sea. And New Almaden—I thought the mountains there were ominous, but I was young, and homesick. They were no more ominous than this green world. Oh, here come the girls, running through the woods to find me. Janet, and Marian, and Evie. Hello darlings! Shall Ganny tell you a story?

It's nice to think that Mary lived with her children and grandchildren in Grass Valley, and then in Hingham, Massachusetts. Young Arthur and his family came to Grass Valley soon after Betty moved east. So Mary was never alone. Solitude, she had that, but she always had someone nearby.

Mary went deaf. She must have felt the isolation. But then, so much of her life was "inside history" as she tells us herself. I'm slightly deaf too. But with my state-of-the-art digital hearing aids, I'll do better than Mary did. I wonder if she sometimes liked the quiet. I do. Sometimes I'd rather not hear the noisy world around me. I can hear enough most of the time. And I don't know what I'm missing. I can only tell the difference when I hear music I know well and it sounds off-key. If I'd never heard it before, I wouldn't be able to tell there was anything wrong, but because I know, I am aware that I'm missing things. It's such a process of diminishment, getting older. But then, one has different joys. Enough remains. And nature—nature lasts. It lasted for Mary. It lasts for me.

I believe that Mary Hallock Foote had experiences of the natural world that partook of the spiritual, the sublime, the transcendental, perhaps even the mystical. These epiphanic moments in nature are hinted at obliquely in her prose, but the prose was written with the reserve of a Victorian lady. Her native reticence prevented her from revealing her deepest feelings to her reading public, except perhaps in veiled form. But those feelings are revealed in her letters, and through them we may come to an understanding of the rapture of her perception and deep knowledge of the landscapes of the West.

In the end, Mary Hallock Foote knew the western landscape like a beloved friend. That she could have felt the way she did about a place that brought her so many disappointments testifies to both the power of the landscape and the depth of her sympathy with the natural world. Let us leave her with her own words of farewell, written in 1891 from the house on the mesa above Boise, the site of both great disappointments and much happiness:

Looking Downstream. Courtesy of Stanford Special Collections, M0115, Mary Hallock Foote Papers, box 17.

> July 18, 1891
> How I wish our delicious nights could reach you, my dearest—"with their odor of sage-brush their breath of balm." Last evening Arthur and I sat out late under the moon and the great bare sky—on our great bare hill, where the grass started and failed because the windmill water would not "go round." The white sun-baked ground, all levelled and graded and rolled in preparation for the lawn that is not—had the effect of a beach in the moonlight—a high beach, impossible but fine, rolling to the edge and disappearing in a dark gulf of invisible land.[22]

The letter was written to Helena, but the image is ours as well, coming downstream to us through more than a century. Thank you, Mary, for giving us the West you knew.

Epilogue

AS I SAID at the beginning of this book, after I wrote my first paper on Mary Hallock Foote I thought I was finished. But I wasn't. Now looking back at the book I have written, I have the same sense that something else needs to be said. I hope that this truly final chapter will somehow bring together all these meandering threads and magically weave them into a tapestry that is, if not smooth, at least whole.

So, what does it mean, all this retrospection into someone else's life? Has it just been a hobby, like classifying butterflies or bird-watching? What has it given me? What have I given it?

One of the most important things for me in doing this work has been that it's taken me home. It's given me back the West in a way I'd have never had it if I hadn't embarked on this particular ride. I thought I was going for a short sail, and it turned out to be a years-long journey. Thomas Wolfe said you can't go home again, and I think that's partly true. You can't go back to the past, which, if you've left a place at a crucial juncture in your life, becomes set in amber, beautiful, untouchable, and unreal. That past is lost but tantalizingly near, forever enshrined with a vision of one's younger, other self. And so, one can't go home, to that home, which has as much substance as a hologram but is as durable as only memory can be. But one does go back to places, and places are real. If I really want to, I can go back to California from London for a long weekend. Whereas Mary could go back to the East only with huge upheaval, expense, time, and trouble. When she traveled she had a week or so of watching the landscape turn from one thing to another to get used to the fact that she was going somewhere else. Nowadays we walk down the thin metal gangway (so light you can feel the wind from that blasted plain of a runway, so fragile you can see the tarmac through the cracks) into a thin metal tube, fight claustrophobia for as many hours as it takes, and arrive in that other world—in my case, a place where the sun is shining and it's still afternoon, when back in London it's midnight.

For many years, when I went back to California with my children, to see my family and to be where I felt like I really belonged, somewhere in myself I thought I'd probably changed too much to ever really be happy there. But then I met Mary, who found herself in California and felt like she didn't belong there. Our stories ran in such parallel lines that I knew I had to explore further. And the work on Mary has taken me to a new old world. Instead of the past, I have a way of being in California now that doesn't have anything to do with nostalgia or childhood, though it's familiar. Similarly, when Mary went back East at the end of her life, she went to a new place, not New York but Massachusetts, and began a new life once again.

So, is that the answer? If one wants to go back, one has to have a new role in the old world. Maybe.

I was thinking about this issue of outward and inward trajectories a few years ago, how one spins out like a wandering satellite. What inspired me was the news that the spacecraft *Voyager* 1, which had then been traveling for thirty-three years, was nearing the edge of the solar system. This fact filled me with a combination of awe and terror; to think of an artificial object, 10.8 billion miles from home, traveling for thirty-three years is something beyond mind-boggling. But think of it—an object, made and touched by human hands, put together by someone who stopped to get a cup of coffee or phone his wife, then returned to tighten a bolt that is still holding fast, out there in space on an odyssey without end.

I've lived in the same house for more than thirty years, and sometimes I find some familiar object in the back of a drawer in the kitchen or upstairs in the attic and think, "Oh that's where it's been," and realize it's been there for ten, maybe fifteen years. So *Voyager,* now in space for nearly forty years, might have been that object in the corner of your parents' garage that just never got moved and now turns out to be your old phonograph from high school, with a Led Zeppelin record still on the turntable.

Voyager carries a gold phonograph record of sounds of earth. So if and when it crashes somewhere, or a wandering starship in some unimaginably distant future finds remains floating around in the emptiness of deep space, someone, some*thing,* will be able to hear what birds and cars and human voices sounded like thousands of years before. That phonograph in your parents' garage will come in handy after all.

The journey of *Voyager* is more than simply the trajectory of an arrow, shot to land who knows where. It has a purpose, though no final destination. Perhaps that is why the whole project inspires such awe. Traveling is one thing, but the idea of traveling endlessly inspires more than awe; it inspires fear and the sense of hanging over a void. Humanity is rooted in the concept of the eternal return.

The instruments on *Voyager,* like an aging person, are failing, one by one. By 2025 nothing will be heard from *Voyager* again. It will then be forty-eight years old and farther from our planet than anything has ever been, or probably ever will be. But its trajectory will continue, even after its messages are silent. Scientists estimate that in about forty thousand years it will pass the constellation Camelopardalis, first noted by Petrus Plancius in the sixteenth century. Who knows whether humanity will still exist in forty thousand years? But something made by humans may still be hurtling through the universe, passing a star seen by a Dutch astronomer a mere half millennium ago and given a human name.

Like Ishmael on the masthead contemplating infinity, *Voyager*'s journey seems like a cosmic metaphor. The contemplation of infinite space is one of Edmund Burke's criteria for sublimity; another is magnitude. The only thing on earth we can compare to the vastness of space is the enormity of the oceans, and our best guide to the oceans is Melville. In *Moby Dick,* Melville states, "Though in many of its aspects this visible world seems formed in love, the invisible spheres were formed in fright."[1] It is this sense of fright, not unmixed with wonder, that has always inspired exploration. *Voyager,* like the *Pequod,* travels through interstellar space in search of its own White Whale—and who knows if it will find it?

A reason why the journey of *Voyager* resonates for me is that we both left earth for the first time in the same month of the same year. Not quite the same day, but close. When *Voyager* left on its mission of discovery of a new old world, I left California on a Pan Am Boeing 747 bound for England. Not quite the reaches of interstellar space, but a new world for a twenty-one-year-old Californian who had never left the West Coast. It was just over a century after Mary Hallock Foote set out for the West for the first time.

While *Voyager* made its Grand Tour, I made mine. When *Voyager* was flying past Amalthea, Io, Europa, Ganymede, and Callisto, I was becoming a European. The years since have seen both of us spin farther and farther away from where we began, *Voyager* passing through unimaginable spaces; me, merely a terrestrial traveler. The years rendered that twenty-one-year-old Californian into another person, who now seems like one of my daughters, whom I have difficulty believing was actually me.

Mary had a similar experience. She talks of her children being westerners; when they went east to school, they longed for Idaho or California. Mary herself says that she loves her West when she is in the East. And her descriptions of western places, many of which I have quoted, reveal an understanding of the numinous qualities of many of those landscapes. Whether or not she wanted to live in them forever, she recognized that certain places have a spiritual integrity of their own, and can change us if we let them. Mary's western experience gave her the tools to transform what might have been an experience of exile into a life of insight and revelation. The West taught her how to read its landscapes, and she in turn gave the world her West.

Like Odysseus making his way home, Mary and I have had adventures along the way. Our Ithacas have hoved into sight, and receded from view, time and again. But as Odysseus found—after the pages of his story were told, when the blind poet stopped speaking and the story of the rest of his life began—it is the journey, and only the journey, that matters in the end.

ITHAKA

As you set out for Ithaka
hope the voyage is a long one,
full of adventure, full of discovery.
Laistrygonians and Cyclops,
angry Poseidon—don't be afraid of them:
you'll never find things like that on your way
as long as you keep your thoughts raised high,
as long as a rare excitement
stirs your spirit and your body.
Laistrygonians and Cyclops,
wild Poseidon—you won't encounter them
unless you bring them along inside your soul,
unless your soul sets them up in front of you.

Hope the voyage is a long one.
May there be many a summer morning when,
with what pleasure, what joy,
you come into harbors seen for the first time;
may you stop at Phoenician trading stations
to buy fine things,
mother of pearl and coral, amber and ebony,
sensual perfume of every kind—
as many sensual perfumes as you can;
and may you visit many Egyptian cities
to gather stores of knowledge from their scholars.

Keep Ithaka always in your mind.
Arriving there is what you are destined for.
But do not hurry the journey at all.
Better if it lasts for years,
so you are old by the time you reach the island,
wealthy with all you have gained on the way,
not expecting Ithaka to make you rich.

Ithaka gave you the marvelous journey.
Without her you would not have set out.
She has nothing left to give you now.

And if you find her poor, Ithaka won't have fooled you.
Wise as you will have become, so full of experience,
you will have understood by then what these Ithakas mean.

—CONSTANTINE CAVAFY
Translated by Edmund Keeley and Philip Sherrard

Notes

Introduction

1. Stegner, *Angle.*

2. Stegner used this term himself at the beginning of *Angle of Repose* in his thanks to "J. M. and her sister for the loan of their ancestors."

3. Foote, *Victorian Gentlewoman.*

4. Hall, *Fair Use.*

5. Copies of Mary Hallock Foote's letters are available in several libraries. The Huntington Library at San Marino, California, Stanford University's Special Collections at the Green Library, and the Lilly Library at Indiana University at Bloomington are the locations I have visited, although the majority of my research was done at the Huntington Library during the summers of 2014 and 2015. In very many cases, the letters are duplicated in all three places. Therefore, rather than list all three, I will identify the letters by date and recipient in the text. However, this letter between Betty Swift and Rosamund Gilder is, as far as I know, only at the Lilly Library in the Gilder archive.

6. The term "safety valve" comes up several times in Mary's letters, the first instance in a letter of September 23, 1873, when Mary was still living at home in Milton. The reference in that instance is to her disappointment at not seeing her friend Helena, who had canceled a visit. The letter in question is long and intense, suggesting that Mary was well aware of the written word's capacity to sublimate emotion.

7. This letter from Mary to Helena was written on the train somewhere along the way, beyond Rock Island, Illinois. There is no date, just "July," but the next letter is written from New Almaden, dated July 18. We know Mary began her journey west on July 5. Mary was in San Francisco a day and a night before traveling to New Almaden, so she probably arrived on the 15th or 16th. That suggests this letter was written at about the halfway point, probably July 9 or 10.

8. Frances Trollope's arch commentary, *Domestic Manners of the Americans,* published in 1832, casts an unsympathetic and rather unimaginative eye over American frontier life, concentrating on the vulgarities and absurdities of its domestic life.

9. Trollope, *Domestic Manners,* fn. 7.

10. Stegner, *Angle,* 104.

11. What Mary actually says is "most brilliant and fascinating young people of their time." *Victorian Gentlewoman,* 103.

12. One letter from Arthur to Mary is signed, "Your big wild loving boy Arthur." In another, dated April 5, 1892, when he was working in Mexico, he writes, "I am

sick for thee tonight. It is hard to go off without a word or hug from thee. Goodnight darling. Thy loving old boy Arthur."

13. Foote, *Edith Bonham,* 153–54.
14. Foote, 321.
15. Letter from Mary to Helena, October 12, 1873.
16. Stegner, *Angle,* 103.
17. Letter from Mary to Helena, October 21, 1876.

Chapter One. In Exile

1. Foote, *Last Assembly Ball,* 39.
2. For a further discussion of this topic, see Gruber, "'The Naturalistic Impulse.'"
3. Kolodny, *Land Before Her.*
4. Foote, "California Mining Camp," 480.
5. Jenkyns, *Victorians and Ancient Greece,* 52.
6. Said, *Reflections,* 173.
7. Said, 173.
8. Said, 173.
9. Said, 174.
10. McCarthy, *Blood Meridian,* 78.
11. Foote, *Victorian Gentlewoman,* 50.
12. Letter from Mary to Helena, October 21, 1876.
13. Letter from Mary to Helena, May 22, 1877.
14. Letter from Mary to Helena, September 3, 1876.
15. Foote, *Edith Bonham,* 77.
16. Foote, *In Exile,* 2
17. In Mary's early story "In Exile," set in a thinly veiled New Almaden, she describes the thoughts of a young mining engineer who has been responsible for the ruination of a beauty spot in the course of his work: "The Engineer's visits to the spring gave him no pleasure, in those days. He felt that he was the inevitable instrument of its desecration" (22).
18. Foote, *Edith Bonham,* 170.
19. Hall, "Brief Look."
20. Letter from Mary to Helena describing her journey west, July 18, 1876.
21. July 18, 1876.
22. Foote, "California Mining Camp," 487.
23. Letter from Mary to Helena, September 24, 1876.
24. Undated letter from Mary to Helena, Santa Cruz, spring 1878. This is one of the few letters that I have seen in only one location, the James Hague papers at the Huntington Library, in what Foote researchers will know as "the shoe box"—a collection of the letters, typed (by whom?) onto file cards, in not quite random order. The box itself is falling apart, held together the last time I saw it, by ribbons!
25. Emerson, *Nature,* chap. 4.
26. *Quaker Faith and Practice,* 5th ed., "Advices and Queries," 1.02, no. 7.

27. Undated letter from Mary to Helena, Saturday, April 1882.

28. Letter from Mary to Helena, Boise, August 30, 1884.

29. Letter from Mary to Helena, Boise Canyon, May 28, 1885.

30. Foote, *Desert,* 51.

31. This idea originates in Darlis Miller's excellent study *Mary Hallock Foote: Author-Illustrator of the American West.*

32. Foote, "Maverick."

33. Foote, *Chosen Valley,* 133.

34. Foote, *Picked Company,* 53.

35. Solnit, *Field Guide.*

36. Foote, *Victorian Gentlewoman,* 29.

37. Letter from Mary to Helena, Victoria, BC, July 5, 1889.

38. Letter from Mary to Helena, Boise, August 25, 1889.

39. Letter from Mary to Helena, Boise, September 15, 1889.

40. Paul, "When Culture Came to Boise," 6.

41. Foote, *Victorian Gentlewoman,* 92–93.

42. Emerson, *Nature,* chap. 4.

43. Foote, *Victorian Gentlewoman,* 329–30.

44. Butala, *Perfection of the Morning,* 55.

45. Foote, *Victorian Gentlewoman,* 275.

46. Foote, *John Bodewin's,* 344.

47. Tuan, "Geopiety," 24.

48. Letter from Mary to Helena, Victoria, BC, May 26, 1889.

49. Armitage, "Illustrator as Writer," 164.

50. Baym, *Women Writers,* 182.

51. Fetterley, *Resisting Reader.*

52. Letter from Mary to Helena, Santa Cruz, October 29, 1877. This letter refers to Arthur's project to make cement, a product unavailable in the region at that time. In one of the ironies that seemed to plague the Foote family, Arthur actually did succeed but got no profit from it as he did not take out a patent.

53. Foote, "Irrigating Ditch," 298–99.

54. Foote, 298–99.

55. Letter from Mary to Helena, Boise Canyon, December 16, 1887.

56. Letter from Mary to Helena, New Almaden, November 5, 1876.

57. Letter from Mary to Helena, New Almaden, September 14, 1876.

58. Letter from Mary to Helena, New Almaden, January 28, 1877.

59. Letter from Mary to Helena, New Almaden, March 1877.

60. Monk, "Approaches," 28.

61. Letter from Mary to Helena, Boise, June 8, 1887.

62. June 8, 1887.

63. A Claude glass is an optical device popular with artists during the eighteenth and nineteenth centuries. It consists of a darkened convex mirror that has the effect of rendering scenes, particularly landscapes, more "painterly."

64. Monk, "Approaches," 24–25.

65. Letter from Mary Hallock Foote to Mary Austin, October 12, 1903. (Mary's handwriting is difficult to read at the best of times. Any errors in transcription of this letter are mine.)

66. Graulich, "Legacy Profile," 48.

67. Letter from Mary to Helena, Boise, October 19, 1894.

68. Letter from Helena to Mary, Santa Cruz, November 1877. This letter, like the letter cited in note 24, is one of the few existing only in the James Hague papers at the Huntington Library. Like that letter, this one is in the "shoebox."

69. Letter from Mary to Helena, Boise, August 19, 1884.

70. Letter from Mary to Helena, Grass Valley, California, March 16. No year, but a note on the transcript of this letter suggests 1896 or 1897. This again is from the "shoebox" at the Huntington. I have not seen it anywhere else.

71. Mary's feelings about Idaho, the toughest and most disappointing of their western homes, reminds me of Solzhenitsyn's thoughts on the topic of experience in *The First Circle:*

> It has long been known that our life stories do not follow an even course over the years. In every human being's life there is one period when he manifests himself most fully, feels most profoundly himself, and acts with the deepest effect on himself and others. And whatever happens to that person from that time on, no matter however outwardly significant, it is all a letdown. (288)

72. Letter from Mary to Helena, Boise, September 15, 1889.

73. Muir, *My First Summer,* ix

74. Letter from Mary to Helena, New Almaden, December 22, 1876.

75. Letter from Mary to Helena, Leadville, Colorado, May 12, 1879.

76. Stegner, *Angle,* 356.

77. Letter from Mary to Helena, Boise Canyon, 1890 (undated).

Chapter Two. New Almaden

1. Letter from Mary to Helena, New Almaden, October 4, 1876.

2. Foote, *Victorian Gentlewoman,* 131.

3. Foote, *Victorian Gentlewoman,* 132. The Italian quotation comes from Dante, *Paradiso* 19:22, the Heaven of Jupiter. "O perpetüi fiori de l'etterna Letizia" (O everlasting flowers of the eternal bliss). I am indebted to Virginia Jewiss for the reference.

4. Sonstegard, "Mary Hallock Foote," 5.

5. Sonstegard, 3

6. Hawthorne, *Scarlet Letter.*

7. Letter from Mary to Helena, New Almaden, December 22, 1876.

8. Foote, *Desert,* 114.

9. Foote, *Desert,* 115.

10. Foote, *Desert,* 125.

11. Foote, *Chosen Valley,* 211.

12. From "The Harshaw Bride," in *A Touch of Sun and Other Stories,* 130.

13. Foote, *Edith Bonham,* 78.

14. Letter from Mary to Helena, July 18, 1876.

15. Kolodny, *Land Before Here,* xii–xiii.

16. Burroughs, "Picturesque Aspects."

17. Foote, *Royal Americans,* chap. 20.

18. Foote, *Royal Americans,* chap. 26.

19. Examples of this phase of Mary's artistic development are seen in the article "Picturesque Aspects of Farm Life in New York," by John Burroughs.

20. Letter from Mary to Helena, March 10, 1877.

21. Said, *Reflections,* 173.

Chapter Three. Leadville

1. Letter from Mary to Helena, Leadville, Colorado, May 12, 1879.

2. Foote, *John Bodewin's,* 50.

3. Foote, 30.

4. Foote, 59.

5. The poem the picture illustrated is the justly forgotten "Bjorn the Bold," by Constantina E. Brooks, a mawkish Christmas ballad of the repentance of a Christianized Viking who goes back to his pre-conversion ways. *Scribner's* 17 (November 1878–April 1879): 313.

6. Foote, *Victorian Gentlewoman,* 115.

7. Letter from Mary to Helena, Milton, New York, Saturday, April 1882.

8. Burke, *Philosophical Enquiry,* 36.

9. Tompkins, *West of Everything,* 71.

10. *Looking for Camp,* in Pictures of the Far West series, *Century* 37, no. 1 (November 1888): 108.

11. *The Coming of Winter,* in Pictures of the Far West series, *Century* 37, no. 2 (December 1888): 324.

12. *Coming of Winter.*

13. Foote, *Victorian Gentlewoman,* 206.

Chapter Four. Mexico

1. Foote, *Victorian Gentlewoman,* 207.

2. Foote, 207.

3. Foote, "Diligence Journey," 1.

4. Foote, 1.

5. Foote, 10.

6. Foote, "Provincial Capital," 328.

7. Foote, 330.

8. Foote, "Trumpeter."

9. Foote, "From Morelia to Mexico City," 647.

10. Xenia is the ancient Greek concept of hospitality, which was required to be shown to guests and travelers. It was a religious as well as cultural obligation.

11. Foote, "Diligence Journey," 1.

12. Foote, 6.

13. Foote, "From Morelia to Mexico City," 643.

14. Letter from Mary to Helena, Boise, May 18, 1893.

Chapter Five. Idaho

1. Letter from Mary to Helena, December 16, 1887.

2. Letter from Mary to Helena, Boise Canyon, April 5, 1885.

3. Luke 10:38-42 (King James Version)

Now it came to pass, as they went, that he entered into a certain village: and a certain woman named Martha received him into her house.

And she had a sister called Mary, which also sat at Jesus' feet, and heard his word.

But Martha was cumbered about much serving, and came to him, and said, Lord, dost thou not care that my sister hath left me to serve alone? Bid her therefore that she help me.

And Jesus answered and said unto her, Martha, Martha, thou art careful and troubled about many things:

But one thing is needful: and Mary hath chosen that good part, which shall not be taken away from her.

4. Letter from Mary to Helena, Boise, October 19, 1894.

5. Smith-Rosenberg, "Female World," 27.

6. Smith-Rosenberg, 28–29.

7. Letter from Mary to Helena, Milton, New York, December 1873.

8. Smith-Rosenberg, "Female World," 15.

9. Letter from Betty Foote Swift to Mary Hallock Foote, September 20, 1924. This letter is in the Gilder Manuscript Collection at the Lilly Library at Bloomington. I have seen it nowhere else.

10. Foote, *Victorian Gentlewoman,* 103.

11. Letter from Mary to Helena, Milton, New York, September 15, 1873.

12. Foote, *Victorian Gentlewoman,* 375.

13. Foote, 131.

14. Letter from Mary to Helena, Boise Canyon, May 28, 1885.

15. Snyder, *Practice of the Wild,* x.

16. *The Winter Camp—A Day's Ride from the Mail,* in Pictures of the Far West series, *Century* 39, no. 1 (November 1889): 57.

17. Foote, *Edith Bonham,* 78.

18. From *Quaker Faith and Practice,* 5th ed., "Advices and Queries."

19. Foote, *Edith Bonham,* 149.

20. Foote, 159.

21. Foote, *Victorian Gentlewoman,* 291.

22. Foote, 299.

23. Foote, 275.

24. Letter from Mary to Helena, Boise Canyon, May 1888.

25. Letter from Mary to Helena, Boise Canyon, June 6, 1885.

26. Letter from Mary to Helena, Boise Canyon, June 1888.

27. Letter from Mary to Helena, Boise Canyon, August 30, 1884.

28. Foote, *Victorian Gentlewoman,* 300.

29. Published in the *Boise Idaho Statesman,* February 24, 1909, and quoted by Mary in her reminiscences (*Victorian Gentlewoman,* 377–78).

Chapter Six. Grass Valley

1. Letter from Mary to Richard Gilder, Grass Valley, July 9, 1896. Unlike the other letters quoted, I have seen this letter only in the Gilder collection at the Lilly, although there are a great number of letters between Mary and Richard Gilder at the Huntington Library, and it is possible that a copy exists there.

2. Miller, *Mary Hallock Foote,* 221.

3. Foote, *Ground Swell,* 43.

4. Stegner, *Selected Letters,* 123.

5. Abrahams, "Real Thing," 96–97.

6. Foote, *Victorian Gentlewoman,* 399.

7. Foote, 400.

8. Foote scholar Christine Hill Smith was, in recent years, given the opportunity to examine these letters through the kindness of Anne Gardiner Brillhart, Mary's great-granddaughter. Sadly, Christie found the letters impossible to decipher. I have looked at them and also found them mainly unreadable.

9. Letter from Mary to Helena, New York, January 13, 1895.

10. January 13, 1895.

11. Letter from Mary to Helena, Boise Canyon, January 20, 1895.

12. Letter from Mary to Helena, Grass Valley, December 17, 1895.

13. Maeterlinck, *Wisdom and Destiny,* 31.

14. Letter from Mary to Helena, Grass Valley, March 22, 1896.

15. Letter from Mary to Helena, Grass Valley, December 6, 1896.

16. Letter from Mary to Helena, Grass Valley, December 22, 1897.

17. Letter from Mary to Helena, Grass Valley, December 30, 1901.

18. Letters from Mary to Helena, Grass Valley, May 18, 1904, October 23, 1904.

19. Letter from Mary to Helena, Grass Valley, June 10, 1910.

20. Foote, "Gideon's Knock."

21. These two letters are only in the Gilder collection at the Lilly Library.

22. Letter from Mary to Helena, the mesa above Boise, July 18, 1891.

Epilogue

1. Melville, *Moby Dick,* 169.

Works Cited

Foote, Mary Hallock

A Victorian Gentlewoman in the Far West: The Reminiscences of Mary Hallock Foote. Edited by Rodman W. Paul. San Marino, CA: Huntington Library, 1972.

John Bodewin's Testimony. Boston: Ticknor and Co., 1886.

The Last Assembly Ball and The Fate of a Voice. Boston: Houghton, Mifflin, 1889.

The Chosen Valley. Boston: Houghton, Mifflin, 1892.

In Exile and Other Stories. Boston: Houghton, Mifflin, 1894.

Coeur d'Alene. Boston: Houghton, Mifflin, 1894.

The Little Fig Tree Stories. Boston: Houghton, Mifflin, 1899.

The Desert and the Sown. Boston: Houghton, Mifflin, 1901.

A Touch of Sun and Other Stories. Boston: Houghton, Mifflin, 1903.

The Royal Americans. Boston: Houghton, Mifflin, 1910.

A Picked Company. Boston: Houghton, Mifflin, 1912.

The Valley Road. Boston: Houghton, Mifflin, 1915.

Edith Bonham. Boston: Houghton, Mifflin, 1917.

The Ground Swell. Boston: Houghton, Mifflin, 1919.

"A California Mining Camp." *Scribner's* 15 (February 1878): 480–93.

"A Sea-Port on the Pacific." *Scribner's* 16 (August 1878): 449–60.

"A Diligence Journey in Mexico." *Century* 23 (November 1881): 1–14.

"A Provincial Capital of Mexico." *Century* 23 (January 1882): 321–33.

"From Morelia to Mexico City on Horseback." *Century* 23 (March 1882): 643–55.

"The Irrigating Ditch." *Century* 38 (June 1889): 298–300.

Pictures of the Far West, I–XI. *Century* 37–39 (November 1888–November 1889).

"Maverick." *Century* 48 (August 1894): 544–50. Reprinted in *The Cup of Trembling and Other Stories,* 1895.

"The Trumpeter." *Atlantic Monthly* 74 (November/December 1894): 577–97.

"Gideon's Knock." In *The Spinners' Book of Fiction.* San Francisco: P. Elder and Co., 1907.

Abrahams, William. "The Real Thing." Review of *Angle of Repose. Atlantic Monthly,* April 1971, 96–97.

Armitage, Shelley. "The Illustrator as Writer." In *Under the Sun: Myth and Realism in Western American Literature,* edited by Barbara Howard Meldrum, 150–74. Troy, NY: Whitson, 1985.

Baym, Nina. *Women Writers of the American West, 1833–1927*. Chicago: University of Illinois Press, 2011.

Burke, Edmund. *A Philosophical Enquiry into the Origins of Our Ideas of the Sublime and Beautiful*. 1757. Oxford: Oxford University Press, 1990.

Burroughs, John. "Picturesque Aspects of Farm Life in New York." *Scribner's* 17 (November 1878–April 1879): 41–54.

Butala, Sharon. *The Perfection of the Morning*. Toronto: Harper Collins, 1994.

Cavafy, C. P. *Collected Poems*. Translated by Edmund Keeley and Philip Sherrard. Edited by George Savidis. Princeton, NJ: Princeton University Press, 1992.

Emerson, Ralph Waldo. *Nature*. 1836. Facsimile of the first edition, with an introduction by Jaroslav Pelikan. Boston: Beacon Press, 1985.

Fetterley, Judith. *The Resisting Reader: A Feminist Approach to American Fiction*. Bloomington: Indiana University Press, 1978.

Graulich, Melody. "Legacy Profile: Mary Hallock Foote." *Legacy: A Journal of American Women Writers* 3, no. 2 (1986): 43–52.

Gruber, Laura. "'The Naturalistic Impulse': Limitations of Gender and Landscape in Mary Hallock Foote's Idaho Stories." *Western American Literature* 38, no. 4 (Winter 2004): 353–73.

Hall, Sands. "A Brief Look at the Literary Life of Mary Hallock Foote." *California State Library Foundation Bulletin*, no. 83 (2006): 2–8.

———. *Fair Use*. Unpublished playscript. 2001.

Hawthorne, Nathaniel. *The Scarlet Letter*. Boston: James R. Osgood and Co., 1878.

Jenkyns, Richard. *The Victorians and Ancient Greece*. Cambridge, MA: Harvard University Press, 1980.

Johnson, Lee Ann. *Mary Hallock Foote*. Boston: Twayne, 1980.

Kolodny, Annette. *The Land Before Her: Fantasy and Experience of the American Frontiers, 1630–1860*. Chapel Hill: University of North Carolina Press, 1984.

Maeterlinck, Maurice. *Wisdom and Destiny*. Translated by Alfred Sutro. Toronto: Musson, 1898.

McCarthy, Cormac. *Blood Meridian or The Evening Redness in the West*. New York: Knopf, 1985.

Melville, Herman. *Moby Dick*. 1851. New York: Norton, 1967.

Miller, Darlis A. *Mary Hallock Foote: Author-Illustrator of the American West*. Norman: University of Oklahoma Press, 2002.

Monk, Janice. "Approaches to the Study of Women and Landscape." *Environmental Review: ER* 8, no. 1 (Spring 1984): 23–33.

Muir, John. *My First Summer in the Sierra*. 1911. Covelo, CA: Yolla Bolly Press, 1988.

Paul, Rodman W. "When Culture Came to Boise: Mary Hallock Foote in Idaho." *Idaho Yesterdays* 20, no. 2 (Summer 1976): 2–12.

Quaker Faith and Practice. 5th ed. "Advices and Queries," 1.02, no. 7.

Said, Edward. *Reflections on Exile and Other Essays*. Cambridge, MA: Harvard University Press, 2000.

Smith-Rosenberg, Carroll. "The Female World of Love and Ritual: Relations between Women in Nineteenth-Century America." *Signs* 1, no. 1 (Autumn 1975): 1–29.

Snyder, Gary. *The Practice of the Wild.* Berkeley, CA: Counterpoint, 2010.

Solnit, Rebecca. *A Field Guide to Getting Lost.* Edinburgh: Canongate Books, 2006.

Solzhenitsyn, Alexander. *The First Circle.* New York: Harper and Row, 1968.

Sonstegard, Adam. "Mary Hallock Foote: Reconfiguring *The Scarlet Letter,* Redrawing Hester Prynne." *Nineteenth Century Gender Studies* 11, no. 2 (Summer 2015). http://www.ncgsjournal.com/issue112/PDF/sonstegard.pdf.

Stegner, Wallace. *Angle of Repose.* New York: Doubleday, 1971.

———. *The Selected Letters of Wallace Stegner.* Edited by Page Stegner. Washington, DC: Shoemaker & Hoard, 2007.

Tompkins, Jane. *West of Everything: The Inner Life of Westerns.* New York: Oxford University Press, 1992.

Trollope, Frances. *Domestic Manners of the Americans.* 1832. London: Century Publishing, 1984.

Tuan, Yi-Fu. "Geopiety." In *Geographies of the Mind: Essays in Historical Geosophy,* edited by David Lowenthal and Martyn J. Bowden. New York: Oxford University Press, 1976.

Index

About the Author

MEGAN RILEY MCGILCHRIST is from Northern California but has lived most of her life in England, where she now teaches English at the American School in London. She has a PhD in American literature from the University of Derby and is the author of *The Western Landscape in Cormac McCarthy and Wallace Stegner: Myths of the Frontier.*